Introduction to Painting Rea...

The secret to painting realistic animals is to take your time and to paint what you see. Study the subject for the color values and the color shapes. Do not be afraid to use strong darks and lights because these are what will give your painting depth. I hope that you will learn some helpful techniques from this book and that you will enjoy your journey through the Bitterroot Backroads where many of these animals live.

About the Author

For as long as I can remember I have been drawing and painting animals. For many years I worked for a large medical corporation and did much of their art work. Having a strong medical background has given me a good understanding of anatomy which helps a great deal when painting any living thing. Later I did portraits for many celebrities and I also did the fine art that was reproduced on about thirty collector plates and figurines. For the past few years I have devoted most of my time to teaching painting and doing workshops. My spare time is spent at home with my family and animals on our small ranch in North Idaho.

For Seminar Information Contact:
Glenice
P.O. Box 224
Hayden Lake, Idaho 83835

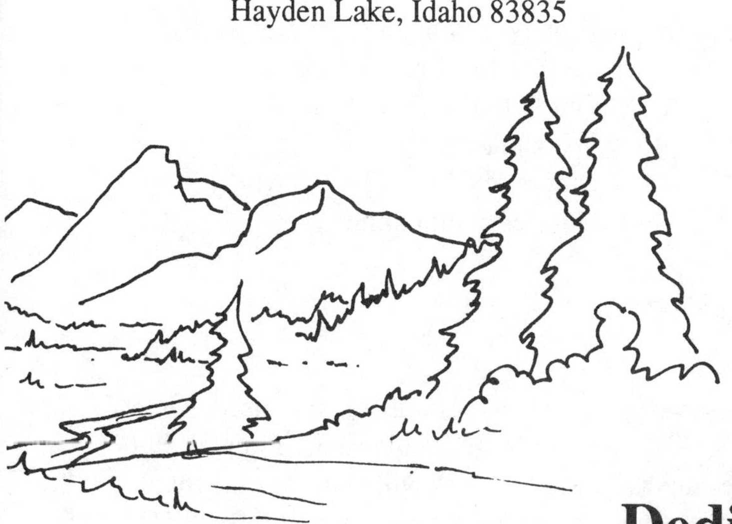

Dedication

This book is dedicated to all of my loyal students and friends who bring me not only ideas for new paintings but photographs of animals. Without their help we would not have some of the animal paintings that I have used in my books and workshops. A special thank you to my little dog Ricky who has traveled so many miles with me to workshops through rain, sleet and snow and as always a special thank you to my Alan.

Paint and Material List

I have listed all of the Paint brands and colors that I have used in this book. I prefer the Shiva Signature Oils because the colors are the closest to natures colors that I have found. I have used this brand for many, many years and have found it to hold up very well. You may use the brands that are available to you or that you are the most comfortable with. You need not rush out to purchase all of the colors that are listed here either. I am sure that you can make do with many of the paints that you have. There are a few colors that I find that I cannot do without and I have put an explanation next to them. If you are not familiar with these colors you may wish to check into them. I am sure that you will enjoy them as much as I do.

Oil Paint

SHIVA SIGNATURE OILS
Ultra White (warm white)
Brilliant Yellow Light (used for white on animals)
Unbleached Titanium (this is a beautiful cream color)
Ice Blue (light blue gray)
Naples Yellow
Raw Sienna
Burnt Sienna
Raw Umber
Burnt Umber
Van Dyke Brown
Paynes Gray (used to make darks)
Ivory Black
Cobalt Blue
Prussian Blue
Shiva Violet Deep
Manganese Blue
Alizarin Crimson
Cadmium Orange
Cadmium Yellow Light
Yellow Citron
Veridian Green
Sap Green
Flesh
Ultramarine Blue
Van Dyke Brown

WEBER PERMALBA
Misty Gray (used for underpainting)
Paynes Gray (used for dark snow)
Cobalt Violet Hue
GRUMBACHER
Thalo Red Rose
Thalo Blue
Thalo Yellow Green
ALEXANDER
Deep Orange
ROWNY GEORGIAN
Brown Madder
GRUMBACHER
Zec Gel

MISCELLANEOUS SUPPLIES
Wipe Out Tool
Binney-Smith 55-11 Palette Knife
Jenkins Sta-Brite Varnish
Graphite Paper
Workable Fixative
Lint Free Cloths (Tee Shirt)
Odorless Turpentine

Canvas

Use the smoothest canvas that you can find. Some artists paint on masonite but it requires some preparation so I use my own brand (GLENICE CANVAS) which is a portrait polyester. You will find it very difficult to achieve fine detail on a rough grade canvas as your brushes will skip over the rough surface and the rough canvas will wear your brushes out very quickly. **NEVER USE CANVAS BOARD.** You may obtain information on where to purchase the GLENICE Canvas or any of the other supplies mentioned in this book from the following distributors:

QUALITY ART
106 W. 31st St.
Boise, Id. 83714
(208) 385-0530

SQUARE GRANNY'S
P.O. Box 97
Athol, Id. 83801
(208) 683-2351

BITTERROOT BACKROADS
P.O. Box 224
Hayden Lake, Id. 83835

CRAFTHOUSE
4193 Hwy. 95 S
Moscow, Id. 83843
(208) 882-1016

Brushes

I have found the brushes that I have listed in this book to work the best for me and the technique that I am trying to teach you in my classes and in this book. They have a nice bounce and hold a good chisel edge and they are not terribly expensive. Some of these brushes are synthetic so they should not be left standing in any cleaning solution. *UNDER NO CIRCUMSTANCE SHOULD YOU APPLY* ANY *KIND OF LARD OR OIL TO THEM.* Applying any of these things to these brushes will take the bounce out of them and they will be ruined. *YOU MUST HAVE GOOD BRUSHES TO DO A GOOD PAINTING. IF YOUR BRUSHES ARE NOT GOOD YOU WILL FIND YOURSELF STRUGGLING WITH THE TECHNIQUE THAT I WILL BE TRYING TO SHARE WITH YOU AND YOU WILL PROBABLY BECOME FRUSTRATED. GOOD BRUSHES AND SMOOTH CANVAS ARE ESSENTIAL IF YOU ARE TO ACHIEVE REALISTIC ANIMALS USING MY METHODS.*

I RECOMMEND:
No. 24 Royal Superb Blend (For all underpainting)
Nos. 2, 4, and 6 Loew Cornell 797-F Series
No. 0 Loew Cornell Mixtique Liner 8050 Series
1 inch and 1/2 inch Langnickle Skywash 1357 Series
1/2 inch Loew Cornell Rake Filbert 7025 Series

General Painting Tips

Painting fur is not difficult if you follow a few basic steps. I cannot stress enough that you either know your subject matter well or that you have good reference material. As well as I know anatomy and animals, I still need to use reference material. The following painting tips may help you.

1. There are three steps to painting fur. If you do not try to skip steps you should not have too much trouble.
   A. Base in all of the color shapes. Use the middle values for this. Do not try to paint hair at this point. The only place that you will make hair strokes is where the hair touches the background. Where two colors meet, soften the edges with a dry brush or with the Skywash.
   B. The second step is to paint in clumps of fur. This is to establish hair length and hair direction. Also work in a little more color at this time. I use the 797-F Nos. 2 and 4 for this step.
   C. The third and final step is to detail the fur and intensify the colors and the darks and lights. Use the No. 0 liner to flip in soft, fine hair on the ends of the clumps that you established in Step Two. Gently soften with the skywash.
   SEE COLOR PLATE FOR THE THREE STEPS IN PAINTING FUR.
2. There are nine values of every color ranging from dark (almost black) to light (almost white). You must give the illusion that these values exist in your animal paintings. You cannot have just dark and light or your work will look flat and will not have depth.
3. Use the appropriate highlight colors and do not be afraid to use reflective light. Remember that all light is not white.
4. Hair grows from the skin out so you should pull your strokes from the skin out. Place the tip of the brush on the canvas and gently press down and as you begin to pull the brush, flip the tip of the brush away from the canvas. When using the liner be sure to keep your paint the consistency of ink.

5. To load the liner, your paint must be like ink. Thin it down by dipping the liner into the clean turpentine and rolling the liner through the paint. Do this each time that you reload the brush. Roll the brush through the paint and pull the brush back at the same time. This will ensure that your brush is well loaded. If the liner is properly loaded you will be able to make many hair strokes. If you get a hair that looks like a pollywog it means that your paint is too thick.
6. Be very careful not to make your hair strokes look straight and stiff. It should look relaxed and soft. See Fig. 1.
7. Do not over load your paint brushes. If you are used to painting with heavier paint then perhaps you should get in the habit of wiping your brush on a cloth before putting it to the canvas.
8. Always use a brush that is compatible in size to the area that you are working on. Using a brush that is too small will give your work a spotty look and if the brush is too large you will not be able to do fine neat work.
9. I use the Skywash brushes to soften my brush strokes and to even out the paint. They come in several sizes but I use the 1 inch and the 1/2 inch the most. A word of caution: Do not over do when you use these brushes or you will blur or wipe out things that you shouldn't.
10. It is very important that the hair direction and hair length are correct. When establishing the hair direction think of a clock with the upper most portion being 12 the right middle being 3, the bottom being 6 and the left middle being 9. See Fig. 2.
11. I brush mix my colors for the following reasons:
    A. I use very little paint and mixing with a knife will waste paint.
    B. I like the variance of color that I get by brush mixing and I find it to be much faster than knife mixing.
    C. If knife mixing is not done correctly it can crush the color pigments in the paint and dull the color.
12. To keep the paint the correct consistency I always dip the tip of the brush into the small container of clean turpentine that I keep by my palette and then I gently blot it on a lint free cloth before going to the paint.
13. Use a soft, clean, lint free cloth such as old tee shirt material. This will work much better than paper towels because it is much more absorbent and it is much easier on your brushes.
14. I never do the eyes first. I feel that you need to be sure that the head is proportioned correctly. For the order in which to paint your animals see Fig. 3.
15. I seldom paint in whiskers. If they are not done properly they can ruin an otherwise very nice painting.
16. After you transfer the pattern onto the canvas you should spray it with Workable Fixative. This will set the lines so that you can paint over them without removing them. Do not, however, overspray or the paint will not want to stick.
17. When your painting is dry to the touch you may want to spray it with a protective finish. I use Jenkins Sta-Brite Varnish. It adds brilliance to the colors and adds depth as well as evening out the finish.
18. I start at the top of the canvas and work down and from the background out. This makes it easier to have more natural looking fur.
19. I do not use mediums and do not recommend them for this technique as they cause the paint to become sticky. I find that just thinning my paint with the turpentine works the best.
20. The best advise that I can give you now is to relax and have fun. Painting realistic animals is a little different than painting landscapes or flowers but once you get these few basic tips down and practice a little you will have a whole new world at your fingertips. I hope that you learn from my book and most of all I hope that you will enjoy doing these lesson plans. These lessons are meant to be used as a guide to learn technique. I hope that you will use what you learn here in your own paintings.

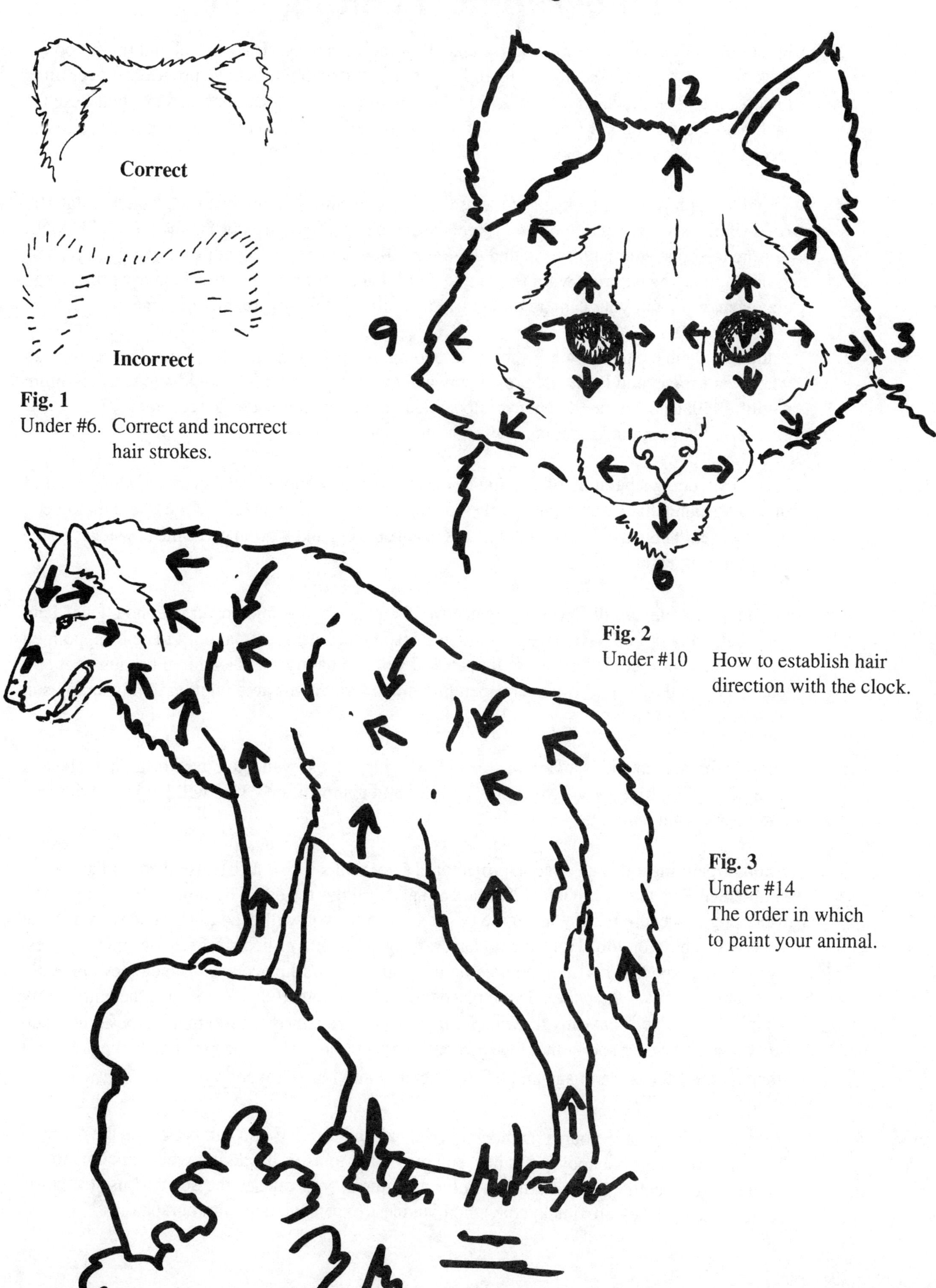

Fig. 1
Under #6. Correct and incorrect hair strokes.

Fig. 2
Under #10 How to establish hair direction with the clock.

Fig. 3
Under #14
The order in which to paint your animal.

Photographic Painting Aids

1. I recommend that my students photograph all of their painting. It is helpful and fun to look back on your work and see how your abilities, talent and techniques have progressed over time. I keep a log book in which I write down all of the brushes, colors and procedures that I use for each painting that I do. I add a photo of the completed painting and this makes an excellent record for me to reflect back on.

   To photograph your work I suggest the use of a 35 mm camera. I prefer to use Kodak Ektar 100 ASA film. I set my painting on an upright easel (as straight as possible) in the OPEN SHADE. Be sure to adjust your painting so that there is no glare and be sure to adjust the focus. It is best to photograph the painting without a frame on it. I also prefer a satin finish on my prints. You may want to mount your camera onto a tripod to eliminate any possible movement.

2. Another valuable painting aid for me is to photograph my own subjects. I carry my cameras whenever I travel and I take pictures of any and everything that I feel could be used in a future painting. I later separate the photos into subject matter groups such as trees, rocks, water, clouds and horses, ducks, bears, adults, children and so on.

   When I am doing a painting of an animal, I gather as many photos as I can of that animal and of the background that I want to use. I then pin all of the photographs to a large board that I keep by my easel. This gives me so many things to chose from and it often gives me new ideas as the painting progresses.

   For photographing wildlife you really need a 35 mm and a 200-600 power telephoto lens. I am sure that many of you have tried to photograph some beautiful animal only to be disappointed when your photos come back from the lab and you can barely see the animal because it is so small. A tripod is helpful if you are spending much time in one area photographing animals in their natural habitat.

   Photography is fun and is an invaluable aid to any artist that wants to create original work. As your photos improve so will your eye for color and composition. This will help you with composing your paintings.

3. Another painting aid is an opaque projector. Many professional artists use them. I have a simple See-Rite that is probably 20 years old and still has the same light bulb in it. I use the following procedure but if you decide to get a projector you will need to practice with it to see what works best for you. I took a wooden drawing board and grided it off into one inch squares. I place the photo that I wish to enlarge on the grid lines and I place a 6 x 6 inch piece of tempered glass over the photo. I then place the projector over the glass. I leave the bottom tray off of the machine. I have my drawing surface set up on an upright easel that can be adjusted up and down and closer and farther away from the projection lens as I need to adjust the projected image size. I focus the image and lightly sketch it and I have saved myself hours of work.

4. You may want to have your reference material enlarged so that you can better see the detail. This may be done on a copy machine. You may want to use a black and white machine to enlarge your picture for a pattern or a color machine so you can see the detail. I use the color copiers because they are quick, convenient and less expensive than photographs.

How to Start Your Painting

These steps are recommended for all of the lesson plans in this book.

1. Make a tracing of the pattern that you want to do. Transfer it onto the canvas by placing graphite paper between the traced pattern and the canvas. Draw over the traced pattern with a stylus or pencil. You may want to anchor the pattern with tape to keep it from moving. Before you remove the pattern from the canvas check to be sure that you have transferred all of the pattern. If the traced pattern that you are transferring has dotted lines on it you do not need to transfer them. They are either for reference or they are for you to reapply that portion of the pattern after you have completed part of the painting.

2. Remove the pattern and spray the canvas lightly with the Workable Fixative. Be careful not to over spray.
   *NOTE: If you should lose part of your pattern when you are painting, let the paint dry and then reapply the pattern. Spray lightly with fixative.

3. Read the "General Painting Tips" prior to painting.

4. Read the instructions on the selected lesson plan completely prior to painting. You may want to highlight colors, brushes or special instructions with a highlighter.

5. Arrange your supplies in a manner that is comfortable for you.

6. Have your reference material where you can refer to it often. This is very important. Rather than tearing up your books, I recommend that you make a zerox copy of the instructions so that you can keep it next to you all of the time and you can keep the book open to the reference picture.

7. Even though the technique that you will been learning in this book is wet on wet, don't expect to complete these paintings in one sitting. They have all been designed as one, two or three day workshops. Learn to take your time. Some of the fine detail is best done on dry paint. AGAIN - RELAX AND ENJOY PAINTING REALISTIC ANIMALS.

8. Be sure that you have good light. I use two adjustable lights on my stand-up easel and three on my drafting table. Remember that the light should come from behind you and from the side, never from the front. It is best to paint with natural North light.

RELAX AND HAVE FUN AND ENJOY YOUR JOURNEY THROUGH THE BITTERROOT BACKROADS.

"Life Mates" Gray Wolves

CANVAS: 14 x 18 Glenice Canvas or Portrait Quality Canvas

PALETTE

Misty Gray
Unbleached Titanium
Raw Sienna
Van Dyke Brown
Cadmium Orange
Cadmium Yellow Light
Sap Green
Paynes Gray
Brilliant Yellow Light
Naples Yellow
Burnt Sienna
Brown Madder
Deep Orange
Thalo Yellow Green
Thalo Blue
Ultra White

BRUSHES

No. 24 Royal Superb Blend
Nos. 2, 4, and 6 Loew Cornell 797-F Series
No. 0 Loew Cornell Mixtique Liner 8050 Series
1 Inch and 1/2 Inch Langnickle Skywash 1357 Series
1/4 Inch Loew Cornell Rake Filbert 7025 Series

MEDIUM

Odorless Turpentine - You will need one container to clean your brushes in and a small container to keep by your palette to be used to thin your paint.

DIRECTIONS

1. Read the sections "General Painting Tips" and "How To Start Your Painting".
2. Read the instructions all of the way through before you transfer your pattern onto the canvas.

BACKGROUND

Give the entire canvas, *EXCEPT THE WOLVES*, a thin even wash of Van Dyke Brown. Skywash to even out the paint and the brush strokes. Add Paynes Gray for the darks in the rock and for the area where the waterfalls go. Add Unbleached Titanium for the light in the rocks and to highlight the tops of the rocks in the waterfall in the foreground. Remember that this is just a wash. Use the No. 24 Royal brush. Make a thin mixture of Sap Green + Paynes Gray and a little Van Dyke Brown and paint in the upper left corner. Work this color down the side of the canvas. Refer to the reference picture. Add more Sap Green to this mixture and paint in the dark area on the right side of the canvas. Do not apply the paint too thick. THIS SHOULD BE APPLIED IN WASHES. Next make a mixture of Sap Green + Deep Orange and paint in the area next to the dark that you just applied. Work towards the waterfall in the background. Next add touches of Cadmium Yellow Light and Cadmium Orange and Thalo Yellow Green. Skywash to soften the colors together.

Add some touches of dark around the rocks in the waterfall being careful not to make the rocks too pronounced. Keep them soft and faint.

WATER IN BACKGROUND WATERFALL

Use the No. 4 757-F and load one side with a small amount of dry Ultra White. Lay the brush on the canvas with the paint side down at the point where the water begins to fall over the rock. Apply a little pressure and as you begin to drag the brush down lift off of the pressure and flip the brush from the canvas. This will let some of the under color show through. Make your water bounce from one rock to the next getting larger in size as it reaches about half way down the canvas. Stop when you are at the wolves hind foot.

"LIFE MATES"
GRAY WOLVES
PAGES 8 - 15

The Three Steps to Painting Fur

1.

STEP ONE:

Use the No. 24 Royal Superb Blend and the 1 inch Skywash. Base in the basic color patterns with a wash of paint. Soften the edges where two colors touch and where the fur touches the background. Skywash.

STEP TWO:

Use the Nos. 2, 4, and 6 797-F and the 1/2 inch Skywash. Intensify the color and establish hair length and direction. DO NOT TRY TO PAINT IN FINE HAIR. Skywash. Use the broad side of the brush to flip one color over the other. This will establish some of the hair strokes.

2.

3.

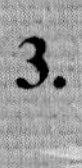

STEP THREE:

Use the Nos. 2, 4, and 6 797-F and the No. 0 liner and the 1/2 inch Skywash. Intensify the color even more. Use the liner to pull the fine hair but do not overdo this. Just paint in enough to give the illusion that there are many. Plant the ends of the fine hair into the fur with the Skywash.

"LIFE MATES" GRAY WOLVES continued

BACKGROUND TREES AND BUSHES

Use the Nos. 2 and 4 797-F brushes to paint in the leaves. Use all of the colors that you used in the background. Use the No. 4 and a mixture of Paynes Gray + Sap Green + a small amount of Thalo Blue to paint in the foliage at the right side of the canvas. Lay the brush on the chisel edge and gently push down to make the leaf shapes. Add some Misty Gray to this mix and paint in a few lighter leaves. Use Misty Gray + Van Dyke Brown to paint in the branches in the dark areas. Make some of the leaves protrude over the water and be sure to keep the colors lighter near the water since that is where the light is coming from. Add branches with Van Dyke Brown. Highlight with Brown Madder + Unbleached Titanium. Mix Brown Madder + Deep Orange and paint in some rust color.

FOREGROUND ROCKS

Use the No. 6 797-F and a mixture of Brown Madder + Misty Gray + Naples Yellow and base in the rocks. Add the darks with Van Dyke Brown + Paynes Gray. Add the highlights with Brown Madder + Naples Yellow + Cadmium Orange. Add more highlights with Deep Orange + Naples Yellow and Deep Orange + Unbleached Titanium.

WATER IN WATERFALL IN FOREGROUND

Rock in waterfall must be dry before painting in water. Study the way that you have laid in the rocks in the waterfall bed. Trace with your finger where you will want your water to fall. Make a mixture of Misty Gray + a touch of Thalo Blue. Follow the same procedure that you used in the background waterfall. After you have established the flow of your water with the dry mixture go back and intensify the color where the water falls over the rocks. You may need to add some darks with Van Dyke Brown + Paynes Gray. Use the same technique that you used to paint in the water only instead of brushing down, lay the brush at the base of the water and push the brush up. This will create the look of a rock under the water. You may want to use the liner and a little Brilliant Yellow Light to add some highlight. Gently Skywash to soften but be careful not to over do this or you will smear all of the water together.

FOREGROUND BUSHES

Base in the bushes with the Nos. 2 and 4 and a mixture of Sap Green + Paynes Gray. Add some highlights with Thalo Yellow Green and Cadmium Yellow Light. Add some touches of Cadmium Orange and Deep Orange + Naples Yellow and Unbleached Titanium.

WOLVES

Give the wolves a wash of Van Dyke Brown + Unbleached Titanium. Skywash. Add darks with more Van Dyke Brown + a little Paynes Gray and add some lights with Van Dyke Brown + Misty Gray. Soften with a dry No. 2. Use the #0 liner and Paynes Gray + Van Dyke Brown to paint in the nose, mouth and to outline the eyes. Underpainting will be eye color.

Add some Brilliant Yellow Light highlights on the faces and add more light on the left side of the females body (the smaller of the two wolves). Add some back light to provide the orange glow around the wolves with Cadmium Orange and Deep Orange + Naples Yellow and Unbleached Titanium. Refer to reference picture.

FINISHING

Add some shadow on the rock under the wolves with a mixture of Paynes Gray + Brown Madder. Apply this with a wash after the rocks have dried overnight.

When the painting is dry to the touch it may be sprayed with Jenkins Sta-Brite Varnish. This will provide a protective coat and bring out the brilliance of the colors.

"LIFE MATES" GRAY WOLVES

"LIFE MATES" GRAY WOLVES

"Grizzly Bear Head"

CANVAS: 14 x 18 Glenice Canvas or Portrait Quality Canvas

PALETTE

Unbleached Titanium
Naples Yellow
Burnt Sienna
Raw Umber
Ivory Black
Sap Green
Turquoise
Brilliant Yellow Light
Raw Sienna
Burnt Umber
Paynes Gray
Ice Blue
Cobalt Violet Hue
Yellow Citron

BRUSHES

No. 24 Royal Superb Blend
Nos. 2, 4 and 6 Loew Cornell 797-F Series
No. 0 Loew Cornell Mixtique Liner 8050 Series
1 Inch and 1/2 Inch Skywash

"GRIZZLY BEAR HEAD"

"GRIZZLY BEAR HEAD"

MEDIUMS

Odorless Turpentine - You will need one container to clean your brushes in and a small container to keep by your palette to be used to thin your paint.

Jenkins Sta-Brite Varnish for your completed painting

DIRECTIONS

1. Read the sections "General Painting Tips" and "How To Start Your Painting".
2. Do not transfer your pattern onto the canvas until you have read the instructions all of the way through.
3. On this particular project you need not transfer each leaf. They may be painted in after the bear is completed. This is also true of the branch. These may be transferred onto the canvas after the painted bear has dried.

STEP ONE:

Starting in the upper left hand corner, use the No. 24 Royal Superb Blend brush and a mixture of Burnt Umber + Ice Blue + a small amount of Cobalt Violet Hue to paint in the background. As you work across the canvas to the right hand corner, add a small amount of Sap Green. Work this mixture down the right side of the canvas to about even with the bear's eyes. Now start adding a small amount of Paynes Gray. Continue adding more as you work to the bottom of the canvas. Now use Paynes Gray + Burnt Umber and paint in the lower left hand corner of the canvas up to the bottom of the bear's muzzle. Skywash with the 1 inch brush.

STEP TWO:

BEAR: Put a transparent wash of Raw Umber over the entire bear. Cover the eyes, nose, etc. Skywash to even out the paint. You should be able to see your pattern through this wash.

Use the No. 6 797-F and start at the top of the bear's back, above his head, and lay in the light hair with Unbleached Titanium. Highlight with Brilliant Yellow Light. Use the chisel edge of the Nos. 4 and 6 to flip the hair strokes out into the background color. Continue working down the shoulders leaving the head and ears unpainted. Gently Skywash in the direction that the hair grows.

As you work down towards the head add Raw Sienna for the gold areas and some Burnt Sienna for the reddish areas. Add Burnt Umber for the dark areas.

NOTE: *REMEMBER TO STUDY YOUR REFERENCE PHOTO. WORK FROM THE OUTSIDE IN AND FROM THE TOP DOWN TO THE EYES (STOP) AND FROM THE BOTTOM UP DOING THE MUZZLE, NOSE AND EYES LAST.*

Use the No. 2 and Brilliant Yellow Light to paint in the light hair around the ears.

Paint the dark area inside the ears with the No. 4 and a mixture of Burnt Umber and Black. Use a dry brush with some of the middle value to paint in the lighter values on the lips and in the dark areas under the eyes.

NOSE

Paint in the entire nose with Raw Umber + Black. Highlight with Ice Blue and highlight the tip of the nose with Brilliant Yellow Light. Use the No. 2 and 4 brushes.

EYE

Outline the eyes with the liner brush and Black. Use the No. 2 and Burnt Umber to paint in the iris. Add touches of Burnt Sienna and Raw Sienna for the lighter areas and highlight with Brilliant Yellow Light.

FINISHING THE FUR

Use the liner to paint in a few fine hairs in the ears and around the eyes and on the muzzle. Gently Skywash to plant these strokes.

BRANCHES

Base in the branches with the No. 4 and Ice Blue. Shade with Raw Umber and highlight with Brilliant Yellow Light. Use the chisel edge of the brush to create the texture in the branch. Vary the pressure on the brush also. Press harder where you want a thicker line and use less pressure where you want a thinner line.

LEAVES

I used Yellow Citron, Sap Green and Naples Yellow as the base colors for the leaves. Add touches of Cobalt Violet, Burnt Sienna and Turquoise to highlight them. You may use any colors that you find pleasing. Use the No. 4 and 6.

FINISHING

When your painting is dry spray it with Jenkins Sta-Brite Varnish to provide a protective coating. This will also bring out the brilliance of the colors and add depth.

Adult Grizzly

"CATALDO ELK"

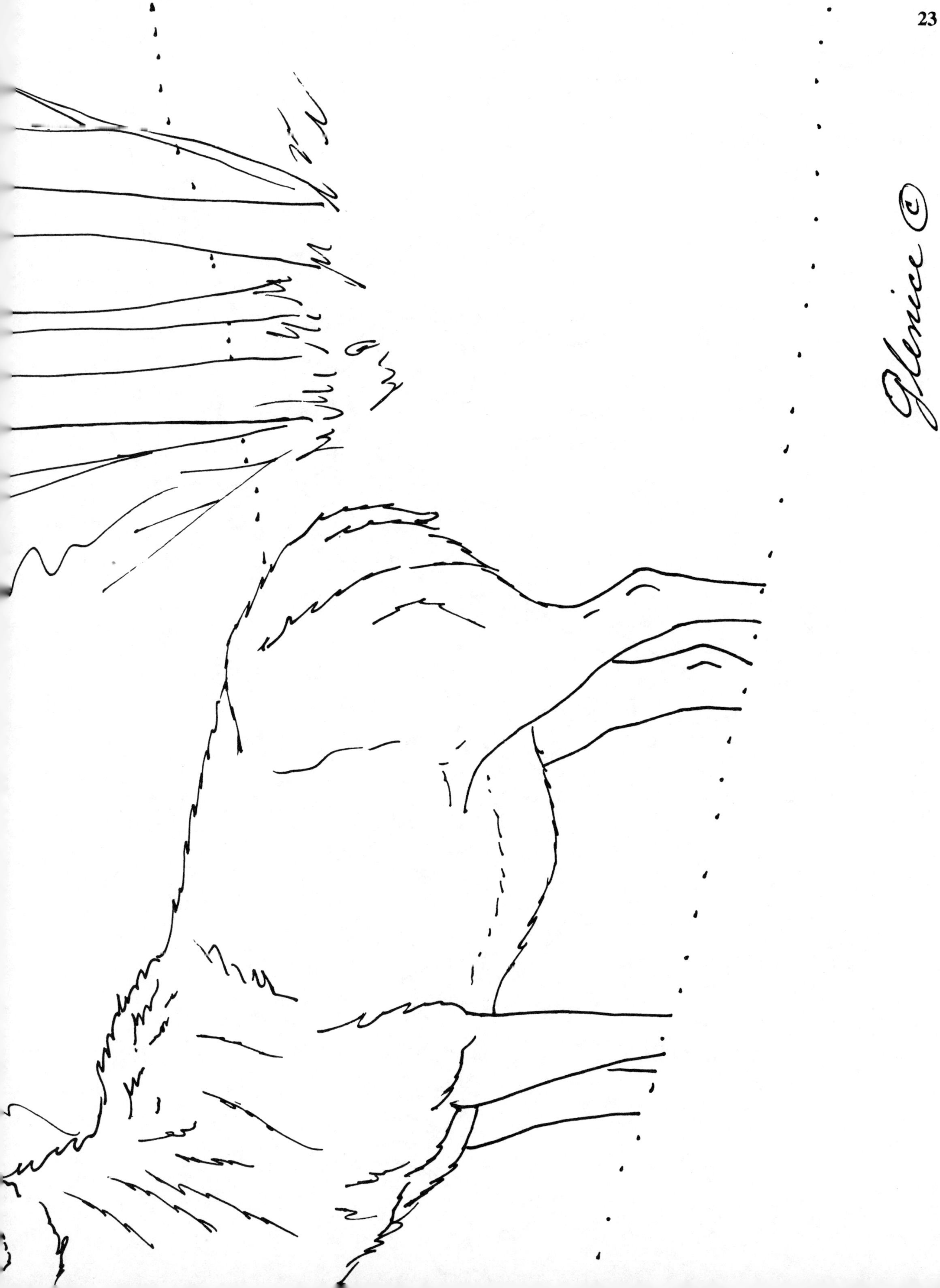

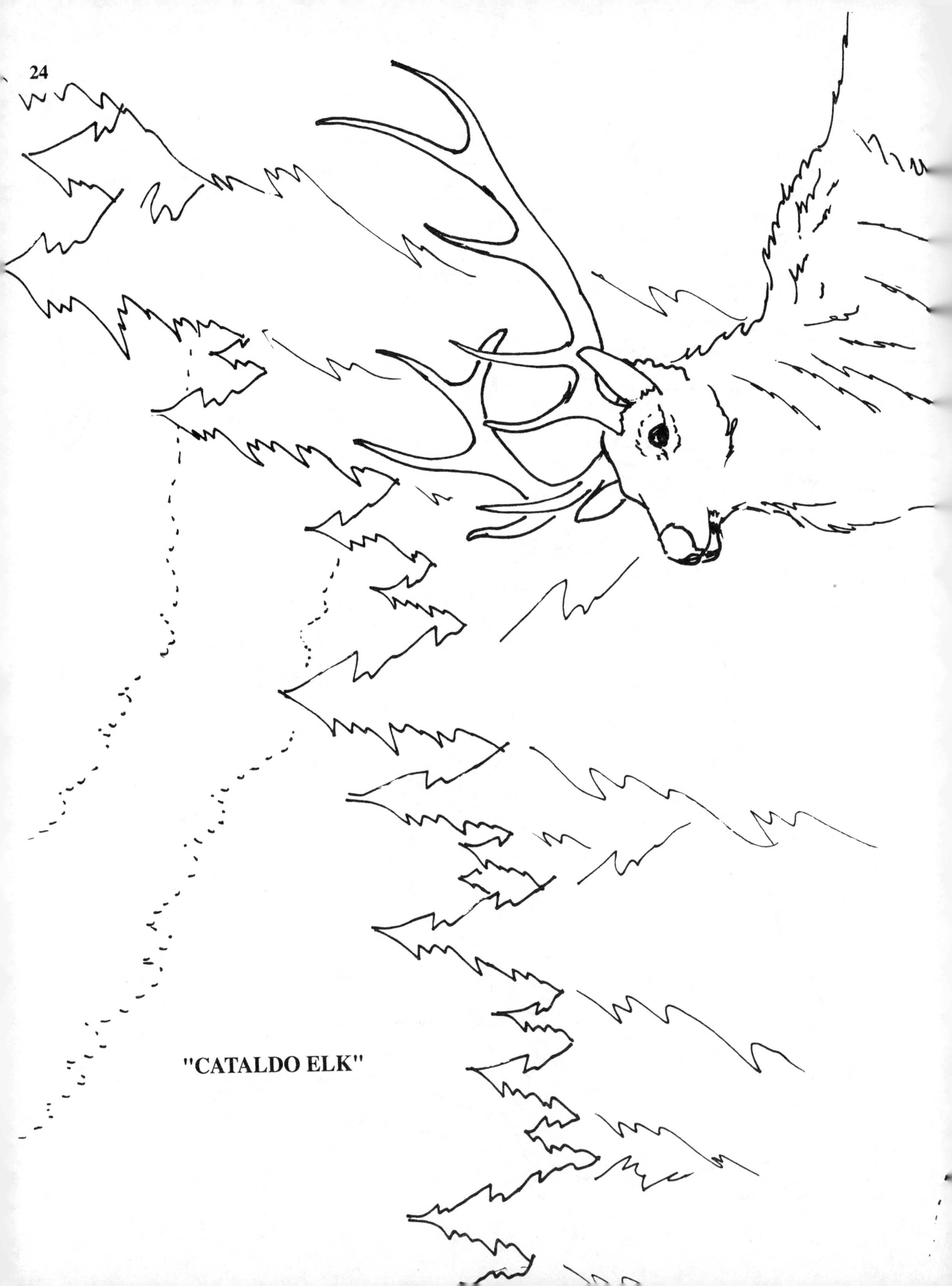

"CATALDO ELK"

"Cataldo Elk"

CANVAS: 14 x 18 Glenice Canvas or Portrait Quality Canvas

PALETTE

Misty Gray
Unbleached Titanium
Burnt Sienna
Raw Umber
Paynes Gray
Cadmium Orange
Manganese Blue
Sap Green
Brilliant Yellow Light
Raw Sienna
Naples Yellow
Burnt Umber
Ivory Black
Cobalt Blue
Shiva Violet Deep
Yellow Citron

BRUSHES

No. 24 Royal Superb Blend
No. 0 Loew Cornell Mixtique Liner 8050 Series
Nos. 2, 4 and 6 Loew Cornell 797-F Series
1/2 Inch Loew Cornell Rake Filbert 7025
1 Inch and 1/2 Inch Langnickle Skywash 1357 Series

SKY

Give the sky and mountain area a thin, even coat of Misty Gray. Skywash to even out the paint.

Mix Cobalt Blue + Manganese Blue and paint in the sky with the No. 24 Royal. Keep the color a little darker at the top of the canvas. Use Misty Gray to tone down the sky color. Paint over the mountain area using a very light value of the sky color. Skywash.

MOUNTAINS

Mix Violet + Misty Gray and paint in the distant mountains. Use a small amount of paint and the paint should be fairly dry. Paint in the ridge to establish the shape and then pull the paint down, leaving some of the misty blue color showing. Skywash to soften.

Mix Violet + Cobalt Blue + Misty Gray to paint in the mountain behind the trees. Do not make the color too intense as it is supposed to be far away. Paint in the ridge and pull the paint down. Go back with the No. 4 and 6 and wiggle in some tree tops. Do not make these too dark or too detailed. You just want to give the illusion that they are there. You may need to add some more Misty Gray for the mist at the bottom of the mountain. Skywash gently.

TREES

Base in the trees with a mixture of Paynes Gray + Sap Green. This mixture should be almost black. Use the Rake Filbert to paint in the tree tops. Use the No. 6 or 24 to pull the paint down. Paint in the dark color in the trees solid. Skywash. Use the Rake and a mixture of Sap Green + Yellow Citron and tap in the tree boughs. Be careful not to part the trees in the middle. Start at the top of the trees and work down letting some of the dark color show through. Do not use too much paint and the paint should not be too thick.

Highlight the right side of the trees with a mixture of Yellow Citron + Brilliant Yellow Light. Apply this color only where the sunlight would hit. Study your reference picture.

GRASS

Base in the grass with Yellow Citron + Unbleached Titanium. Use the Rake to flip the grass up into the trees so that you do not have a hard edge. Use the No. 24 to paint in the grass area. Paint down to the bottom of the elk's legs. DO NOT LEAVE A STRAIGHT EDGE. Use the broad side of the brush to flip the paint into the unpainted area. You will paint in the foreground later. Use the Wipe Out Tool to wipe out the small twigs in the background and to wipe out the area where the birch tree will go. Start at the base of where you want your tree and push the tool to the top of the canvas. If you want a thicker tree repeat the procedure. Use the longer end of the tool and wipe it on a cloth after each stroke.

"GRIZZLY BEAR HEAD"
PAGES 16 - 21

"FORGOTTEN THUNDER "
PAGES 36 - 41

CATALDO ELK continued

BIRCH TREES

Use the No. 4 or 6 to base in the trees with Misty Gray + a small amount of Burnt Umber. Use the No. 4 and mixture of Cobalt Blue + Misty Gray + Paynes Gray to paint in the dark side of the trees. Place the chisel edge on the edge of the tree and lightly pull it around the tree trunk, lifting off the canvas as you near the middle of the tree trunk. Load only one side of the brush and do not use thick or heavy paint. Paint in the left side of the trees using the same technique and Brilliant Yellow Light. Add some reflected light on the dark side of the tree with a mixture of Cobalt Blue + Misty Gray. Use the No. 0 liner and a mixture of Burnt Umber + Paynes Gray to paint in the eyes in the tree trunks. Highlight with Brilliant Yellow Light. Add some small branches and some saplings at the base of the trees. If you did this with the wipe out tool you need only add some highlights.

GRASS

Detail the grass behind the elk. Use the Rake Filbert and the No. 0 liner. Add some different colors by mixing Sap Green with any of the other colors on your palette. Use the Brilliant Yellow Light and the Unbleached Titanium for the lightest areas. Be sure to keep the paint the consistency of ink when using the liner and be sure to keep your grass strokes loose and relaxed. Grass does not stick straight up like it has been starched. Refer to the reference picture often.

ELK

Start with the antlers. Use the No. 2 and a mixture of Raw Umber + Misty Gray to base them in. Add Paynes Gray to this mix for the darks and then highlight them with Brilliant Yellow Light. You will use the No. 0 liner for this.

Base in the dark areas on the elk with the No. 4 and a mixture of Raw Umber + Paynes Gray. Use this mix for the mane on the neck and on the legs also. Base in the body area with Unbleached Titanium + Raw Umber and a touch of Burnt Sienna. Use a very dry brush and a touch of the dark mixture to paint in the muscles and the dark hair clumps on the body area. Use the No. 2 to clump in the hair and the lighter hair in the mane. Watch the hair direction and hair length. Highlight the body with Brilliant Yellow Light. Study the reference picture.

Paint in the glow around the entire animal with Brilliant Yellow Light. Add a little Cadmium Orange next to the Brilliant Yellow Light. Detail the face with Black + Raw Umber for the dark areas and some of the base body color around the eye. Use Unbleached Titanium + Brilliant Yellow Light + a small amount of Raw Umber for the rump. Add a little of the dark mixture to define the tail.

NOSE AND EYE

Use the No. 0 liner and Black to paint in the nose and the eye. Highlight with Brilliant Yellow Light. Use Unbleached Titanium for the light area on the chin.

GRASS AND SMALL TREES

Paint in the small trees in the background if you did not use the wipe out tool. Use Misty Gray + Raw Umber. If you did use the tool, just add touches of color.

Paint in a few leaves on the birch trees with the No. 2 and Sap Green + Yellow Citron. Add some touches of Burnt Sienna and Cadmium Orange. Finish the grass in front of the elk by basing in a mixture of Unbleached Titanium + Naples Yellow + a small amount of Yellow Citron. Use the Rake Filbert to make grass and also the No. 0 liner to flip in the longer grass strokes. Paint in the dead branch with Burnt Umber + Paynes Gray. Highlight with Brilliant Yellow Light and Unbleached Titanium.

FINISHING

Spray with Jenkins Sta-Brite Varnish when the painting is dry.

"Blue Fantasy"

CANVAS: 14 x 18 Glenice Canvas or Portrait Quality Canvas

PALETTE

Misty Gray	Ultra White
Brilliant Yellow Light	Thalo Red Rose
Thalo Blue	Cobalt Blue
Paynes Gray	Burnt Umber

BRUSHES

No. 24 Royal Superb Blend
Nos. 2, 4, and 6 Loew Cornell 797-F Series
No. 0 Loew Cornell Mixtique Liner 8050 Series
1/2 Inch Loew Cornell Rake Filbert 7025 Series
1 Inch and 1/2 Inch Langnickle Skywash 1357 Series

MEDIUM

Odorless Turpentine - you will need one container to clean your brushes in and a small container to keep by your palette to be used to thin your paint.

DIRECTIONS

1. Read the sections "General Painting Tips" and "How To Start Your Painting".
2. Before you transfer your pattern onto the canvas to be sure to read he instructions all the way through.

BACKGROUND

Give the entire canvas a thin even coat of Misty Gray and then Skywash to even out the paint and the brush strokes. The paint should be thin enough that you can see your pattern lines. Use the No. 24 Royal.

Make a mixture of Ultra White + Cobalt Blue + Thalo Blue and paint in the area behind the horse. Keep your colors soft and misty. Add some darker values in the upper corners by adding a small amount of Paynes Gray to the blue mix. Continue down the sides. Refer to the reference picture. Skywash to soften. Add some touches of Thalo Red Rose above the horse and soften with the Skywash.

Use the rake filbert and some of the light blue mix + Ultra White and tap in the pine trees. Add some of the pink trees with the Thalo Red Rose + Ultra White. Do not overload this brush. It might be wise to load only one side and then gently wipe the loaded brush on a cloth to be sure that the tip of the brush separates. Gently Skywash to soften the trees and to set them back.

SNOW

Use the No. 24 Royal to paint in the snow with a mixture of Thalo Blue + Cobalt Blue+ Ultra White. Skywash to even the paint out. Darken the lower corners with the snow mix + Cobalt Blue + Thalo Red Rose. Skywash to soften the colors together but do not overblend. Add highlights with Ultra White. Add touches of Thalo Red Rose. Skywash.

GRASS

Use the rake filbert and a mixture of Cobalt Blue + Thalo Blue + Paynes Gray to lightly paint in some grass. Bring in some lighter grass strokes with lighter blue and some of the pink tones.

HORSE

Base in the entire horse with the Nos. 2, 4 and 6 797-F brushes and a mixture of Misty Gray + Cobalt Blue. Keep this base coat very light in color. Add the darker areas by adding Paynes Gray to the base mixture. You may want to add a little Cobalt Blue also. Add touches of Thalo Red Rose and Skywash. Highlight with Ultra White. *DO NOT PAINT IN THE MANE AND TAIL YET.*

EYES, EARS AND NOSE

Use the #0 liner to outline the eyes and nostrils with a mix of Paynes Gray + Burnt Umber. Add a little Misty Gray to contour the nostrils. Fill in the eyes with the dark mixture and highlight the eyes and nostrils with Brilliant Yellow Light. Paint in the inside of the ears with the dark mixture and highlight with Brilliant Yellow Light.

MANE AND TAIL

Use the No. 4 and a very dry mixture of Misty Gray + Cobalt Blue. Dry brush the mane and tail in using the chisel edge to flip the ends of the hair. Add touches of pink and highlight with the No. 0 liner and Ultra White.

FINISHING

Add final highlights with Brilliant Yellow Light. Paint in hooves with some of the pinkish blue color and plant the hooves into the snow. Use the liner to pull a few fine grasses.

When painting is dry it may be sprayed with Jenkins Sta-Brite Varnish.

Appaloosia Colt

"BLUE FANTASY"

Glenice ©

"BLUE FANTASY"

"Forgotten Thunder"

CANVAS: 18 x 24 or 20 x 24 Glenice Canvas or Portrait Quality Canvas

PALETTE

Unbleached Titanium
Ice Blue
Ultra White
Paynes Gray
Burnt Sienna
Burnt Umber
Veridian
Sap Green
Ivory Black
Brilliant Yellow Light
Misty Gray
Prussian Blue
Raw Sienna
Raw Umber
Naples Yellow
Thalo Yellow Green
Alizarin Crimson

BRUSHES

No. 24 Royal Superb Blend
Nos. 2, 4 and 6 Loew Cornell 797-F Series
No. 0 Loew Cornell Mixtique Liner 8050 Series
1 Inch and 1/2 Inch Skywash 1357 Series
1/2 Inch Loew Cornell Rake Filbert 7025 Series

MEDIUMS

Odorless Turpentine - You will need one container to clean your brushes in and a small container to keep by your palette to be used to thin your paint.

DIRECTIONS

1. Read the sections "General Painting Tips" and "How To Start Your Painting".
2. Do not transfer your pattern onto the canvas until you have read the instructions all of the way through.

BACKGROUND

Give the entire canvas a coat of Misty Gray. Skywash.

SKY

Paint in the sky with the No. 24 Royal and a mixture of Ice Blue +Prussian Blue + Paynes Gray. Keep the upper right hand corner a little darker. Add Ultra White to lighten. Refer to the reference picture often. Skywash.

TREES

Mix Veridian + Paynes Gray + Prussian Blue and a little of the sky mixture for the base coat on the trees. Use the Rake Filbert to lightly tap in the tree shapes. Go back and add Paynes Gray to darken and add Misty Gray to lighten.

Glenice ©

"FORGOTTEN THUNDER"

"FORGOTTEN THUNDER"

PRAIRIE

Study the reference picture to see how the colors of the prairie are in layers. Put them in and leave them alone. If you over work these areas you will have a muddy build up of paint DO NOT BLEND. Use the No. 24 Royal and a mixture of Raw Sienna + Misty Gray to paint in the area under the trees. Next mix some Sap.Green + Unbleached Titanium and paint in the next layer of color. Next is Burnt Sienna + Raw Sienna + Misty Gray. Add some Thalo Yellow Green to this for the gold areas. Work down to the area just below the fighting buffalo and stop. The reddish area under the buffalo is Burnt Sienna + Misty Gray and a touch of Alizarin Crimson. Now gently Skywash. Do this just enough to soften. Continue working down the canvas to the bottom using the same colors. As you near the bottom of the canvas intensify the colors but be careful not to make them too vibrant. Add a little Veridian at the bottom. Skywash.

FIGHTING BUFFALO

Start with the buffalo on the left, by painting in all of the dark areas with Raw Umber + Unbleached Titanium. Paint in the darkest darks by adding Paynes Gray to this mix and paint in the lights by adding more Unbleached Titanium. The gold on the mane is Unbleached Titanium + Naples Yellow and a touch of Raw Umber. The buffalo on the right is done the same way using Raw Umber + Paynes Gray for the darks. Add Ice Blue to lighten and use Misty Gray for the lightest areas. Add Raw Sienna to the light mix for the mane. Use the Nos. 2 and 4. Paint in the eyes, noses and horns with Raw Umber + Ice Blue. Highlight with Misty Gray and add Ivory Black to define the detail.

BIG BUFFALO

Use the No. 24 Royal and paint in the darks with a mixture of Raw Umber + Paynes Gray. This should be a transparent wash but do not make it runny. Be sure to pull hair strokes into the background colors. Paint all of the darks in on the head and add lights with Misty Gray + Unbleached Titanium. DO NOT OVER BLEND OR OVER PAINT. For the mane use Raw Sienna + Burnt Sienna + Misty Gray and some of the dark mixture. Apply this with a thin coat of paint. The area at the top of the hump will be lighter and the colors will darken as they come down towards the shoulder. Study the reference picture. Paint the light area with Unbleached Titanium + Ice Blue. Soften with the Skywash. Do not over blend. Do not do the eye yet.

DETAILING

TREES - Go back to the trees and use the No. 2. Paint in some tree trunks with Raw Sienna and add darks with Raw Umber. Detail some of the darks and lights in the foliage. Add just enough to establish some depth. Keep the colors muted because they are in the distance.

PRAIRIE - Use the No. 0 liner to paint in some grass strokes. Do just enough to give the illusion that there is a lot of grass. Watch the length. You can use the Rake Filbert for this. Use the No. 2 to tap in some flower shapes. Keep them soft and muted. Use whatever colors you like for this.

FIGHTING BUFFALO - Clean up the darks and lights. Intensify some of the darks by adding a little Ivory Black. Paint in the shadow underneath the buffalo with a mix of Burnt Sienna + Alizarin Crimson + Prussian Blue. Use this mix that has been thinned down to paint in the dust clouds.

BIG BUFFALO - Paint in the dark crevices in the fur with Raw Umber + Paynes Gray for the lighter areas and use Ivory Black for the darkest areas. Make a bluish color with Paynes Gray + Misty Gray + some Prussian Blue and paint in some of the highlights. Keep your strokes loose and relaxed. Even though buffalos have course hair, it is soft and should not look stiff when they are painted. Add more Misty Gray to highlight around the eyes and on the nose. Put in the brown area under the eye with Burnt Umber + Raw Sienna. You may wish to add a touch of Burnt Sienna. Start at the bottom of the

DETAILING

BIG BUFFALO continued

canvas and work up the shoulder and from the canvas edge work in towards the neck. Start laying in the darks again and then work in the lights with Burnt Sienna + Raw Sienna. Work dark to light. Highlight the clumps of fur with Unbleached Titanium + Naples Yellow. As you work up the shoulder, the darks will get lighter as will the lights. Work up to Brilliant Yellow Light in the lightest areas and Raw Umber in the dark areas. Skywash. Use the liner to paint in some tiny curly hairs.

EYE - Use the liner and Ivory Black to outline the eye. Base in the iris with the No. 2 and Burnt Umber. Darken the pupil with Black. Add some Raw Sienna and Burnt Sienna to contour. The reflected light is Ice Blue and the highlight is Brilliant Yellow Light.

FINISHING

When the painting is dry it may be sprayed with Jenkins Sta-Brite Varnish.

Cow Buffalo & Calf

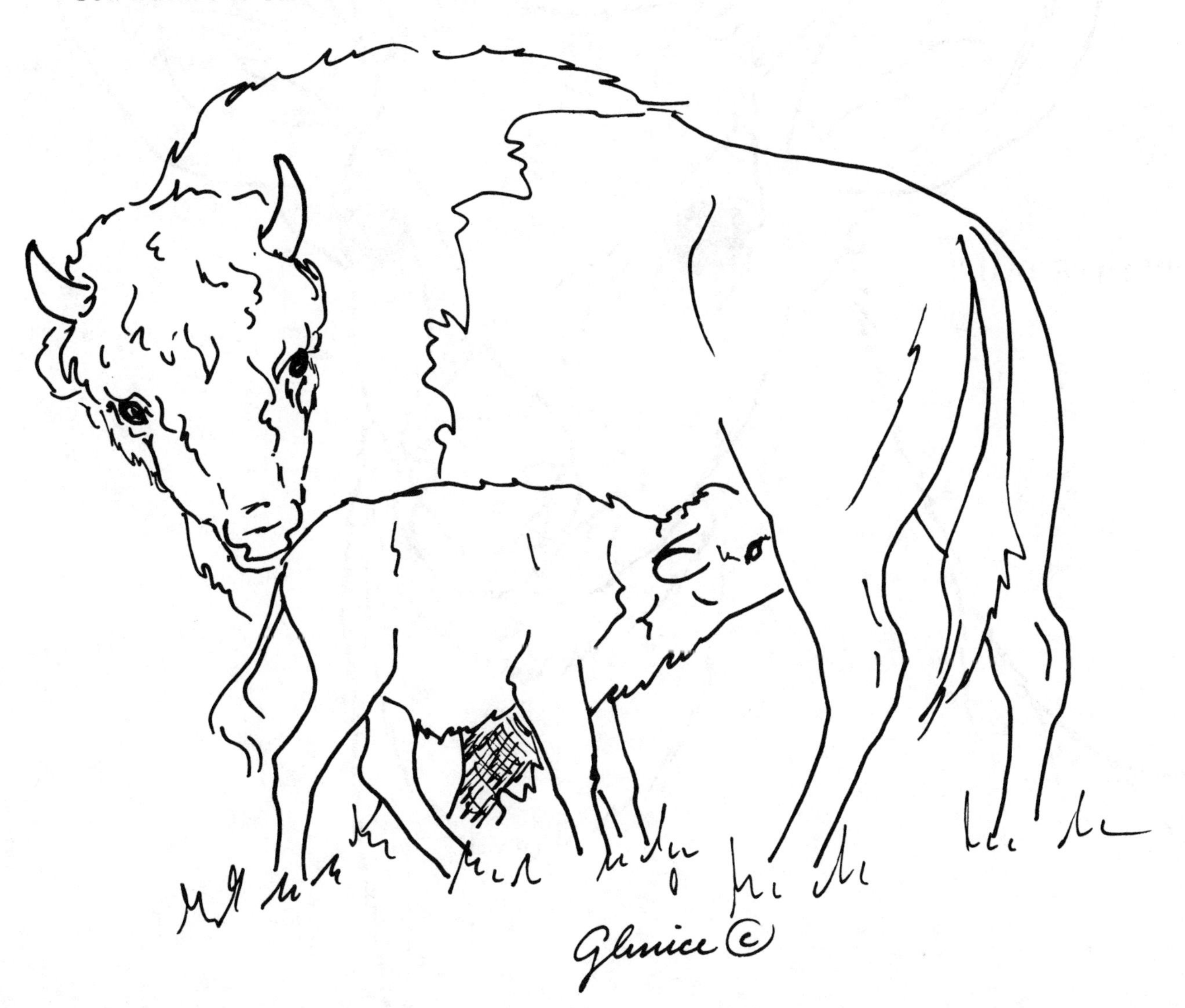

"WHITE TAIL"

Glenice ©

"White Tail"

CANVAS: 9 x 12 Glenice Canvas or Portrait Quality Canvas

PALETTE
Sap Green
Brilliant Yellow Light
Ultra White
Raw Sienna
Burnt Umber
Paynes Gray
Unbleached Titanium
Naples Yellow
Burnt Sienna
Cobalt Blue

BRUSHES
No. 24 Royal Superb Blend
Nos. 2, 4 and 6 Loew Cornell 797-F Series
#0 Loew Cornell Mixtique Liner 8050 Series
1 Inch and 1/2 Inch Skywash 1357 Series
1/2 Inch Loew Cornell Rake Filbert 7025 Series

MEDIUMS

Odorless Turpentine - You will need one container to clean your brushes in and a small container to keep by your palette to be used to thin your paint.

DIRECTIONS

1. Read the sections "General Painting Tips" and "How To Start Your Painting".
2. Do not transfer your pattern onto the canvas until you have read the instructions all of the way through.

BACKGROUND

Use the No. 24 Royal and a mixture of Sap Green and Paynes Gray to paint in the upper corners and down the sides of the canvas. Use Sap Green + Brilliant Yellow Light for the center above the deer's head. Skywash. Use the X stroke to work the darks and lights together.

DEER

Base in the deer with No. 24 and the No. 2 and 4 797-F brushes and a mixture of Unbleached Titanium + Burnt Umber. Add Paynes Gray for the darker areas. Add more Burnt Umber + Paynes Gray for the dark areas on the ears, forehead and muzzle.

Use the chisel edge of the brush and very little paint. You can use this brush with no paint on it at all and lift paint off to make hair also. Paint in the white on the neck and the muzzle with Ultra White. The shaded areas are Ultra White + Cobalt Blue. Use Unbleached Titanium around the eyes and highlight with Brilliant Yellow Light. Work in some Raw Sienna and Burnt Sienna on the face and the ears. Use Unbleached Titanium + Burnt Umber for the long ear hair. Base these in with the No. 2 and detail with the No. 0 liner.

EYES AND NOSE

Outline the eyes with Burnt Umber + Paynes Gray and the No. 0 liner. Use the No. 2 to fill in and add a touch of Burnt Sienna in the lower right corner of the eyes. Highlight with Brilliant Yellow Light.

Base in the nose the same as the eyes. Add a little Unbleached Titanium to the dark mixture to contour and highlight with the Brilliant Yellow Light.

PINE BOUGHS

Use the Rake Filbert and a mixture of Sap Green + Paynes Gray to tap in the pine boughs. If this is done on wet paint, use the Skywash. If the background paint is dry be very, very gentle with the Skywash step. Add Brilliant Yellow Light to the Sap Green for the light areas.

"WHITE TAIL"continued

ANTLERS

Base in the antlers with the No. 4 and a mixture of Unbleached Titanium + Burnt Umber + Raw Sienna. Add darks with base mixture + Paynes Gray. Highlight with Unbleached Titanium and use Brilliant Yellow Light for the tips.

FINISHING

Add some reflected light along the top of the neck and on the left ear with Cobalt Blue + Ultra White.

When the painting is dry it may be sprayed with Jenkins Sta-Brite varnish. This will provide a protective coating and add depth and brilliance to your work.

"WHITE TAIL"
PAGES 42 - 44

"HIGH MOUNTAIN MEADOW"
PAGES 50 - 55

"Morning Glow"

MEDIUM

Odorless Turpentine - You will need one container to clean your brushes in and a small container to keep by your palette to be used to thin your paint.

DIRECTIONS:

1. Read the sections "General Painting Tips" and "How To Start Your Painting".
2. Read the instructions all of the way through before you transfer your pattern onto the canvas.

BACKGROUND

Use the No. 24 Royal Superb blend to cover the background with a mixture of Paynes Gray + Thalo Blue + Sap Green. Add a little Misty Gray to lighten the color as you move towards the center of the canvas. Use an "X" stroke, being sure that you overlap the strokes. Keep the upper left corner darker as well as the left side of the canvas and the portion in front of the coyote.

Skywash to even out the paint, but do not work all of the color variations out by over blending. Using the 1/2 inch rake filbert and a mixture of Thalo Blue + Paynes Gray + Ultra White tap in some light areas to indicate pine boughs. Skywash to blur and soften. Repeat until you reach a look that you like.

SNOW

Base in the snow with the Nos. 6 and 4 with a mixture of Thalo Blue + Ultra White + a touch of Paynes Gray. Add more Ultra White to lighten and add highlights with Ultra White. Use the liner to tap in the tiny snow crystals. STUDY THE REFERENCE PICTURE.

TREES

Base in the dark part of the tree branches with the No. 4 and a mix of Raw Umber + Paynes Gray. Add some lighter bark with Raw Umber + Misty Gray. Add the snow on the branches using the same colors as above.

COYOTE

Base in the coyote with the a wash of the background colors. Add touches of Raw Sienna and Burnt Sienna and highlight the chest and face with Ultra White. Refer to the reference picture often for color placement and variation. Use the Nos. 2 and 4 for blocking in the fur and use the liner for fine hair. Outline the eyes, nose and mouth with Paynes Gray + Raw Umber. Paint in the eyes with Raw Umber + Brilliant Yellow Light and a touch of Sap Green. Use Brilliant Yellow Light to highlight the eyes, nose and to make the teeth. Use the liner to add the fine highlight hairs of the left side with Ultra White. Add some reflected light on the right side of the head, neck, back and legs with Ultra White + the blue snow mix. **VERY GENTLY SOFTEN WITH THE 1/2 INCH SKYWASH.**

TREE ON RIGHT

Base in the tree on the right side the 1/2 Inch rake Filbert and a mixture of Paynes Gray + Sap Green + Thalo Blue. Be sure that the mix is a darker value than the background. Add more Paynes Gray to darken and add Ultra White to lighten. Use the liner to add the brightest highlights with Ultra White. If the color will not lighten enough use some Brilliant Yellow Light. Gently skywash.

FINISHING

When the painting is dry, spray with Jenkins Sta-Brite Vanish.

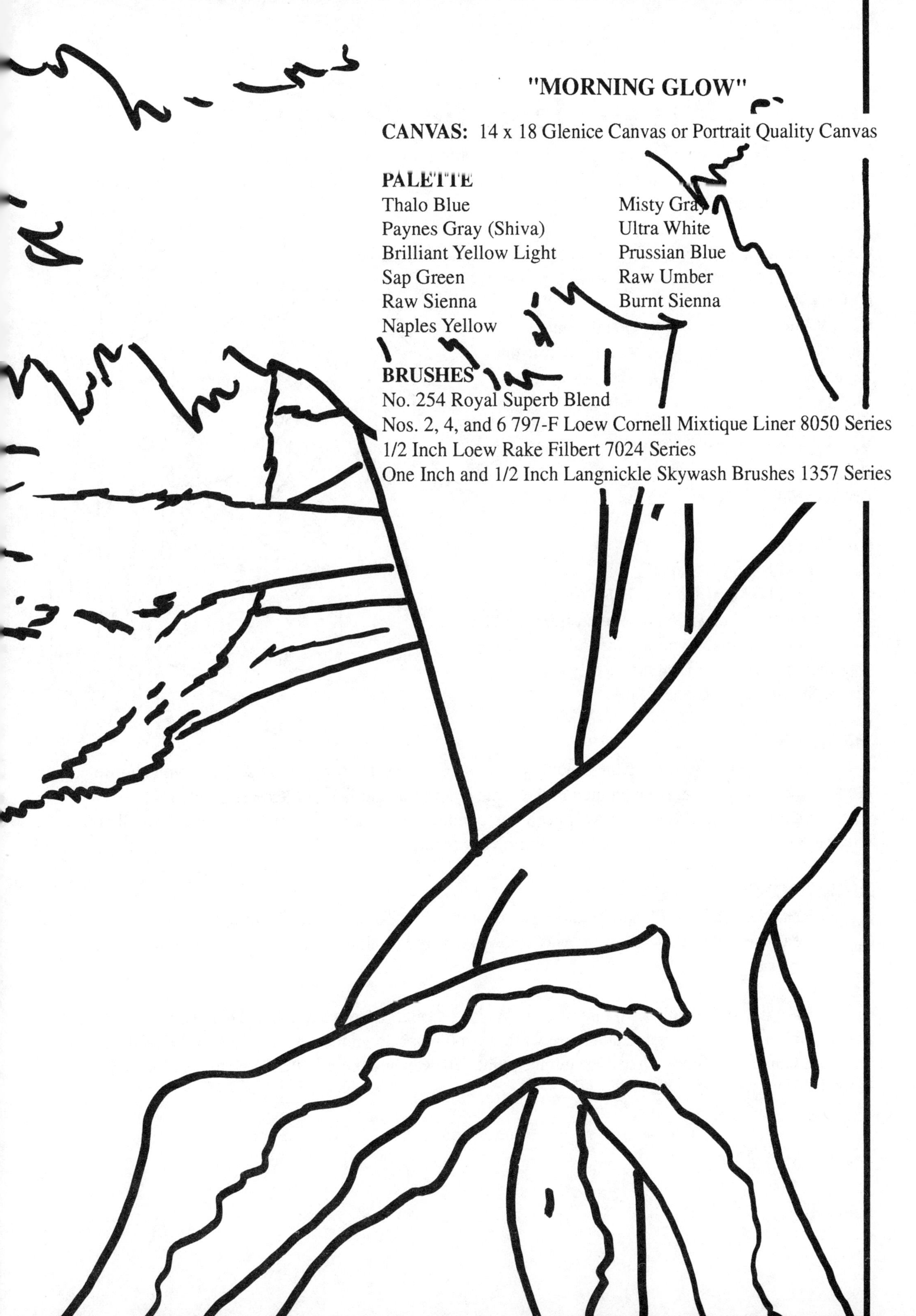

"MORNING GLOW"

CANVAS: 14 x 18 Glenice Canvas or Portrait Quality Canvas

PALETTE

Thalo Blue	Misty Gray
Paynes Gray (Shiva)	Ultra White
Brilliant Yellow Light	Prussian Blue
Sap Green	Raw Umber
Raw Sienna	Burnt Sienna
Naples Yellow	

BRUSHES

No. 254 Royal Superb Blend
Nos. 2, 4, and 6 797-F Loew Cornell Mixtique Liner 8050 Series
1/2 Inch Loew Rake Filbert 7024 Series
One Inch and 1/2 Inch Langnickle Skywash Brushes 1357 Series

"High Mountain Meadow"

***NOTE:** I painted this painting using the paint horses but I have included patterns for elk and bear that may be used instead. The instructions for painting these animals are at the end of the following instructions.

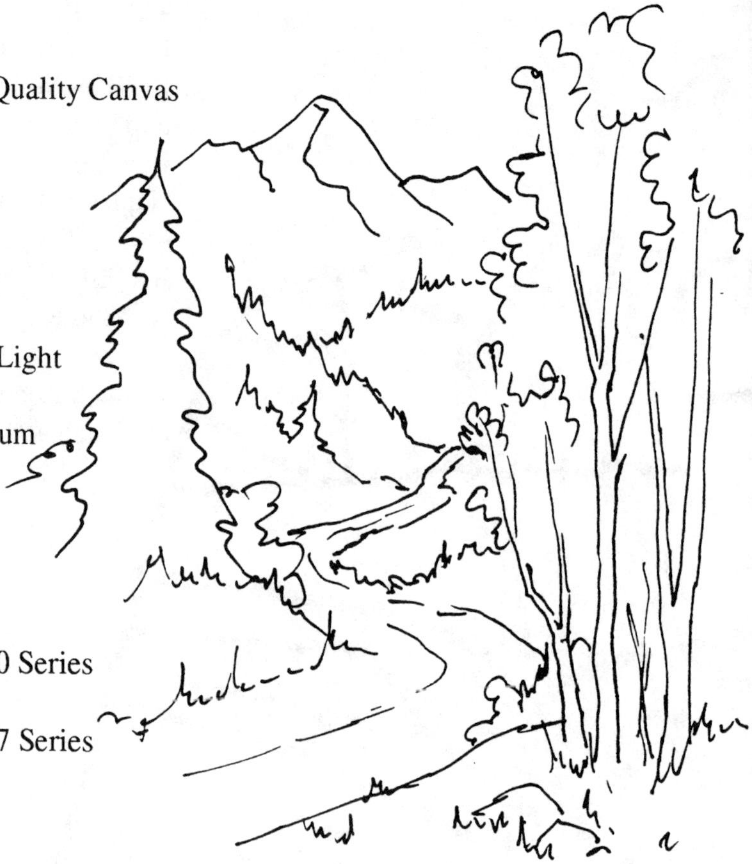

CANVAS: 14 x 18 Glenice Canvas or Portrait Quality Canvas

PALETTE

Ultra White
Thalo Blue
Paynes Gray
Flesh
Thalo Yellow Green
Raw Sienna
Burnt Umber
Brilliant Yellow Light
Cobalt Blue
Alizarin Crimson
Misty Gray
Sap Green
Cadmium Yellow Light
Burnt Sienna
Unbleached Titanium

BRUSHES

No. 24 Royal Superb Blend
Nos. 2, 4 and 6 Loew Cornell 797-F Series
1/2 and 1/4 Inch Loew Cornell Rake Filbert 7520 Series
No. 0 Loew Cornell Mixtique Liner 8050 Series
One Inch and 1/2 Inch Langnickle Skywash 1357 Series
Binny-Smith 55-11 Palette Knife

MEDIUMS

Zec Gel - Use to texture the mountains. It is not necessary for you to use this if you choose not to. The mountains may be painted in the same colors that are listed in the lesson plan.

Odorless Turpentine - You will need one container to clean your brushes in and a small container to keep by your palette to be used to thin your paint.

DIRECTIONS:

1. Read the sections "General Painting Tips" and "How To Start Your Painting".
2. Read the instructions all of the way through before you transfer your pattern onto the canvas.

SKY

Base in the sky with a mixture of Ultra White + Cobalt Blue + a touch of Thalo Blue. Keep the upper corners a little darker and add more white as you work down the canvas. Paint 1/3rd of the way down the canvas and Skywash to even out the paint. You can add more Ultra White to the blue mix and scrub in a few wispy clouds.

MOUNTAINS

Mix Misty Gray + Paynes Gray + Alizarin Crimson to make a purple gray color. Use the No. 4 or No. 6 797 F to paint in the mountain shapes. Drag the paint down the canvas from the top of the mountains. DO NOT add more paint. Skywash to soften the bottom edge of the paint. This will help establish the mist at the base of the mountain range. Use the palette knife to chop the ZEC into the flesh color. Do not use the flat of the knife to mash the paint! Use the edge of the knife and gently chop until the gel and the paint are well mixed. Make a bead of paint along the knife edge and apply the highlights to the mountains. Remember where your light source is coming from and only apply highlights to that side of the mountains. Make ragged edges rather then straight lines. Let your mountains rest. We will add the snow later after the paint has had a chance to set up. Feather out the bottom edge of the paint again with the Skywash brush.

BACKGROUND TREES

Use the dark mountain mix + Sap Green and a touch of Alizarin Crimson. Use the No. 4 797-F and wiggle in the tree shapes with the chisel edge of the brush. Hold it in a vertical position and as you wiggle it up and down drag it across the canvas. Be very careful not to make the tree line too even. This is in the high mountains so don't be afraid to make mountains. The tree line should be uneven. Refer to your reference picture.

SHRUBS

Study the reference picture. Add some Cadmium Yellow Light to the above mixture and paint in some shrubs. Mix Sap Green + Cadmium Yellow Light for a different value and add more bushes. Keeping your light source in mind, add highlights with Thalo Yellow Green.

FOREGROUND TREES

With a mixture of Sap Green + Paynes Gray use the chisel edge of the No. 4 797-F and indicate where your large trees will be. Place the brush at the base of the tree and draw it up towards the top in one smooth even stroke. Lift off of the pressure as you near the top of the tree. Don't be afraid. Do not paint in any more on your trees at this point.

FOREGROUND

Use the No. 24 Royal and Sap Green + Cadmium Yellow Light and paint in the grassy foreground. This is when you will establish where your creek will go. Your paint should not be very thick. Add your rock shapes with the No. 4 and a mix of Burnt Umber + Misty Gray. Use the sky color to paint in the river down to where the waterfall starts. Mix Raw Sienna + Burnt Umber and paint in a WASH over the lower stream bed. Darken this mix with more Burnt Umber and paint in the area where the waterfall is. Add some rocks in the river bed. Shade them with Burnt Umber and add highlights with Raw Sienna + Unbleached Titanium. Let this part of the painting dry completely before applying a glaze of Sap Green + Cobalt Blue and a touch or Thalo Blue. This glaze may be made by adding linseed oil to your paint or you may use Glazing Gel of just plain turpentine to make your paint transparent. **BE SURE THAT YOUR PAINTING IS DRY BEFORE APPLYING THE GLAZE.** Add the ripples and the white on the waterfall with Ultra White. Use the No. 4 and the No. 0 liner for this.

SNOW

Mix Ultra White and ZEC in the same manner that you used before and add the snow on the mountains. You may need to add some dark on the shadowed side of the mountain with Paynes Gray + Misty Gray + Cobalt Blue. Use the Nos. 2 and 4 for this. Use the 1/2 inch Skywash to **VERY GENTLY** soften the edges together.

TREES

Use the 1/4 inch rake filbert and Sap Green + Paynes Gray and paint in the trees in the middle ground. Highlight them with various shades of light green. Add the highlights on the right side of the trees. Add some Cobalt Blue + Misty Gray on the left side of the trees. Continue with the same colors and technique and do the large trees in the foreground and the grass. Use the 1/2 inch rake filbert for these. Add bushes with Sap Green + Paynes Gray and add highlights and reflected light with the blue mix. Add a little Raw Sienna + Unbleached Titanium to indicate the path and also to establish the river bank. Shade with Burnt Umber.

ROCKS

Add some Burnt Umber + Paynes Gray to shade the rocks. Add some Raw Sienna + Unbleached Titanium to highlight and some Cobalt Blue + Misty Gray for the reflected lights on the left side of the rocks.

OPTION

ELK
for Mountain Meadow

Should be placed on the far bank. Buck should be close to waterfall.

"HIGH MOUNTAIN MEADOW"

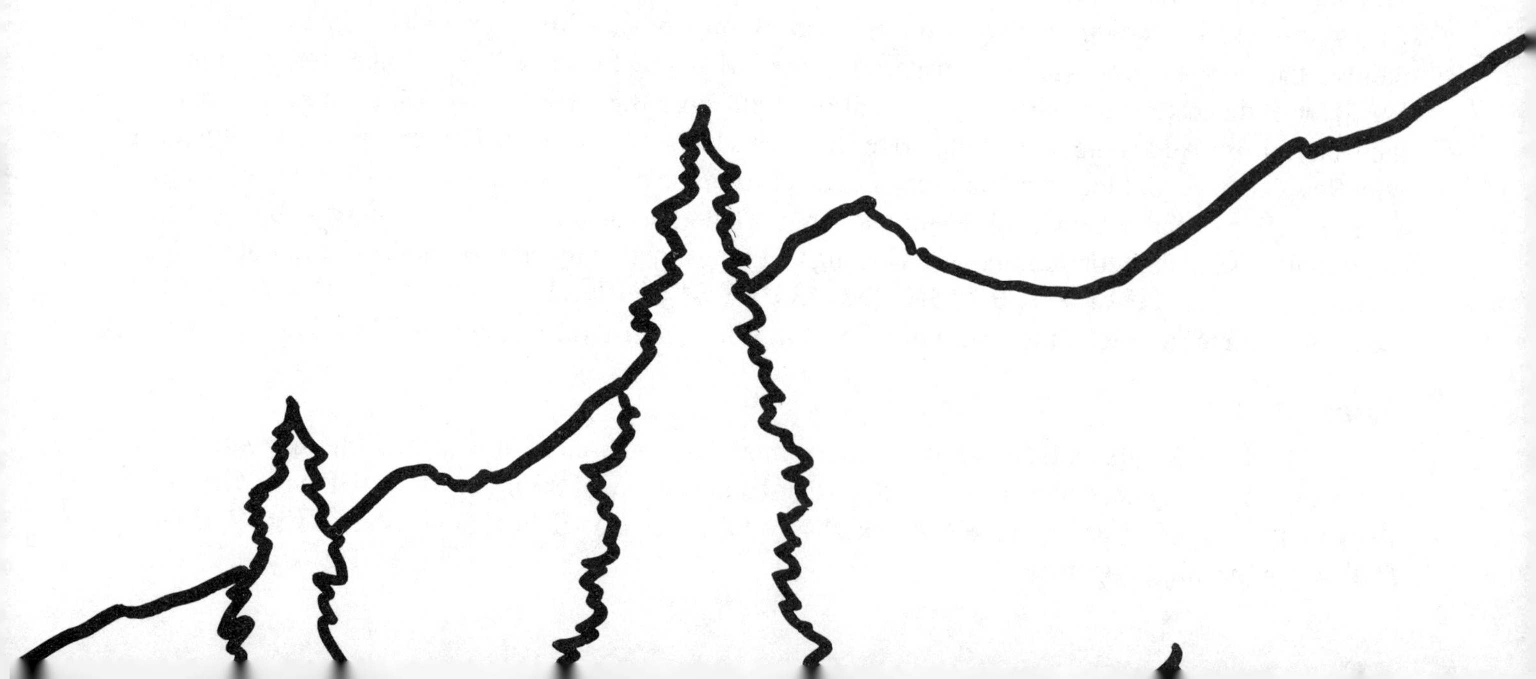

HORSES

You may paint your horses any color that you wish, I liked the look of the paint horse. I used Raw Sienna + Burnt Sienna and Burnt Sienna + Burnt Umber and Raw Sienna + Unbleached Titanium for my spots and Ultra White for the light parts. Use the No. 2 797-F and the No. 0 liner

ELK

Base in with Burnt Umber for the darks and Raw Sienna + Unbleached Titanium for the light areas. The rear of the elk is Unbleached Titanium. Add shadow with Burnt Umber and highlight with Brilliant Yellow Light and Unbleached Titanium.

GRIZZLY BEAR

Base in the entire bear with Burnt Umber + Raw Sienna + a touch of Burnt Sienna. Add darks in the shadowed areas with Burnt Umber + Paynes Gray. Highlight with Unbleached Titanium + Raw Sienna.

FINISHING

Whatever animals you use, you will need to pull some grass up over their feet. Spray with Jenkins Sta-Brite Varnish.

OPTION **GRIZZLY BEAR**
for Mountain Meadow

Bear should be placed on far bank and to the right of the waterfall.

"HIGH MOUNTAIN MEADOW"

"Here Kitty Kitty"
Cougar

CANVAS: 16 x 20 Glenice Canvas or Portrait Quality Canvas

PALETTE

Misty Gray
Ultra White
Naples Yellow
Burnt Sienna
Prussian Blue
Sap Green
Brilliant Yellow Light
Unbleached Titanium
Raw Sienna
Van Dyke Brown
Paynes Gray (Permalba)
Veridian Green

BRUSHES

No. 24 Royal Superb Blend
Nos. 2, 4 and 6 Loew Cornell 797-F Series
No. 0 Loew Cornell Mixtique Liner 8050 Series
1/2 Inch Loew Cornell Rake Filbert 7520 Series
1 Inch and 1/2 Inch Langnickle Skywash 1357 Series

MEDIUM

Odorless Turpentine - You will need one container to clean your brushes in and a small container to keep your palette to be used to thin your paint.

DIRECTIONS

1. Read the sections "General Painting Tips" and "How To Start Your Painting".
2. Before you transfer your pattern onto your canvas be sure to read the instructions all the way through. It is not necessary to transfer the dotted lines on the pattern. These areas will be painted in with a very thin and soft valued paint and the lines will show through.

BACKGROUND

Give the entire canvas a thin, even coat of Misty Gray. Use the No. 24 Royal. Skywash to even out the paint. Work in some Permalba Paynes Gray across the top of the canvas. Do not paint a straight line. Pull the strokes down from the top of the canvas so that you have a feathery edge. Skywash. Next add some Raw Sienna for the goldish area above the trees. This requires a very small amount of paint. Skywash. Begin adding some Paynes Gray + Sap Green making very faint tree top shapes. Do not use very much paint on your brush and the paint should be rather dry. You may want to add a little Prussian Blue. Skywash.

As you work down to the snow, darken your mixture to almost a black value. Also darken the right side of the canvas where the big tree will go. DO NOT USE HEAVY PAINT. Skywash.

ROCKS

Use the No. 2, 4 and 6 brushes lightly loaded with Van Dyke Brown to paint in the rocks. Highlight with Raw Sienna + Unbleached Titanium. Keep the rocks darker at the bottom by adding a bit more Van Dyke Brown. You may need to add some Paynes Gray also. Add some touches of Misty Gray and Brilliant Yellow Light to some of the rocks being careful not make all of the shapes the same.

SNOW

Base in snow with Ultra White + a touch of Prussian Blue. If too bright, add a touch of Paynes Gray.

Add Brilliant Yellow Light to lay in the highlights. Intensify some of the shadows with Misty Gray + Paynes Gray and a touch of Prussian Blue. Keep your light source in mind when you are painting in the shadows and highlights. The light is coming from above.

TREES

Add the trees in the background by using the rake filbert and a very small amount of paint. Use Paynes Gray + Sap Green + a little Veridian. Skywash. Work from the back trees forward. Darken the trees as you come forward. The big tree at the right should be almost black. Soften the base of each tree by pulling the snow up and into the branches. Soften all with the Skywash. Go back over the trees with a mixture of Misty Gray + Prussian Blue and a touch of Veridian. Use the rake brush and lightly tap this mixture in. This will create the snow on the branches. Highlight with Misty Gray.

CAT

Use the Nos. 2 and 4 and a mixture of Raw Sienna + a dab each of Burnt Sienna and Van Dyke Brown. Cover the entire cat. Add the shadowed areas by adding more Van Dyke Brown to the mixture. Add small amounts of Burnt Sienna for the reddish areas. Add some Naples Yellow for the highlighted areas. Go back and paint the highlight with Unbleached Titanium. Be sure to soften the edges of the colors so that there is a gently blending. You do not want to make spots. Paint in the cream colored areas with Ultra White + Van Dyke Brown. Add some Paynes Gray or Prussian Blue for the shaded areas. Intensify all of the darkest areas with pure Van Dyke Brown.

NOSE

Base in the nose with Burnt Sienna + Misty Gray. Add Paynes Gray + Van Dyke Brown for the darks.

EYE

Outline the eyes and the pupil of the eye with the dark mixture. The underpaint will provide the eye color.

DETAILING

You may go back and add some fine hair strokes on the cat. Use the No. 0 liner. Add Ultra White to highlight the white areas. Do not overdo this step and be careful of hair length.

FALLING SNOW

Lay the painting flat on a piece of paper and use the No. 24 Royal brush. Make a mixture of Misty Gray + Paynes Gray + White. This mixture should be quite loose but not runny. Hold the brush in one hand and lightly tap the handle on your other hand. Hold the brush about eight inches from the painting. You should probably try this on a piece of paper first. If the mixture is too loose you will get large runny flakes and the paint will splatter in bunches. Experiment to find the correct consistency.

FINISHING

When the painting is dry, it should be sprayed with a protective coating. I use Jenkins Sta-Brite Varnish.

"HERE KITTY KITTY"
COUGAR

Glenice ©

"HERE KITTY KITTY"
COUGAR

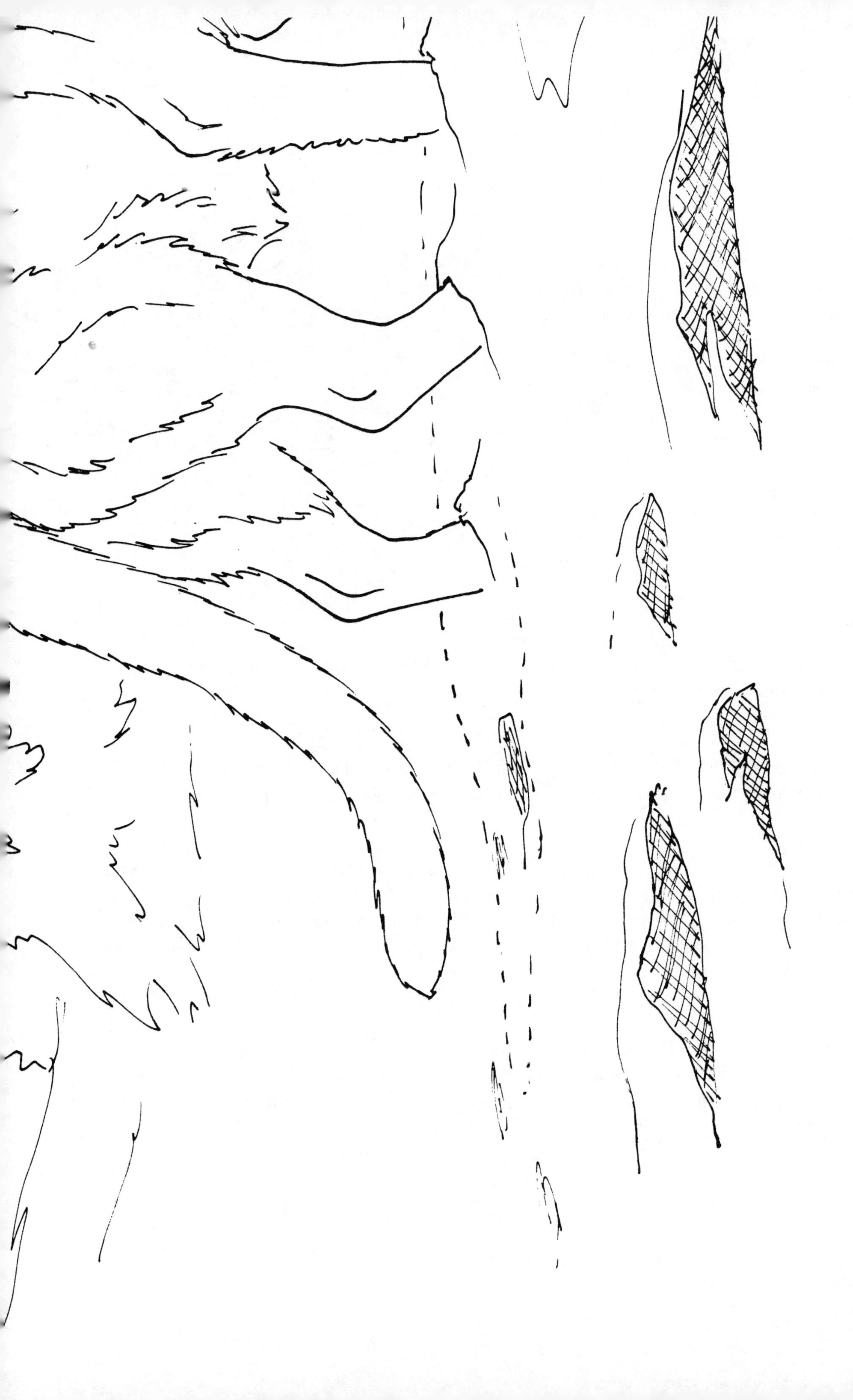

"Flower"

CANVAS: 12 x 16 Glenice Canvas or Portrait Quality Canvas

PALETTE

Misty Gray
Briliant Yellow Light
Naples Yellow
Raw Sienna
Paynes Gray (Shiva)
Alizarin Crimson
Sap Green
Ultra White
Unbleached Titanium
Burnt Sienna
Burnt Umber
Ivory Black
Cobalt Blue
Cadmium Yellow Light

BRUSHES

No. 24 Royal Superb Blend
Nos. 2, 4 and 6 Loew Cornell 797-F Series
No. 0 Loew Cornell Mixtique Liner 8050 Series
1 Inch and 1/2 Inch Langnickle Skywash 1357 Series

MEDIUM

Odorless Turpentine - You will need one container to clean your brushes in and a small container to keep by your palette to be used to thin your paint.

DIRECTIONS:

1. Read the sections "General Painting Tips" and "How To Start Your Painting".
2. Read the instructions all of the way through before you transfer your pattern onto the canvas.

BACKGROUND

Use the No. 24 Royal to base in the dark green areas with a mix of Sap Green + Paynes Gray. This should be almost black. Base in the log with Burnt Umber + Raw Sienna + Misty Gray. This will be your middle value. **DO NOT PAINT IN HARD EDGES AROUND THE SKUNK.** Use the flat edge of the brush and flip in towards the skunk to give a fuzzy look. It will be much easier to paint in the hair than if you leave a hard edge.

LEAVES

Use the Nos. 4 and 6 797-F brushes and Sap Green + Cadmium Yellow Light to base in the leaves. Use different values to create depth. Use the liner to paint in some small stems. Use the chisel edge of the No. 4 to paint in some of the ferns. Highlight some of the edges with Cadmium Yellow Light + Brilliant Yellow Light.

FLOWERS

Use the No. 4 to base in the flowers with Cadmium Yellow Light + Ultra White. The centers are Burnt Sienna + Alizarin Crimson and a little Cadmium Yellow Light. Use the No. 4 and Alizarin Crimson and a little Cadmium Yellow Light. Use the No. 4 and Alizarin Crimson + Ultra White for the pink buds and flowers.

"FLOWER"
PAGES 62 - 67

"SKIPPY THE
GRAY SQUIRREL"
PAGES 68 - 70

SKUNK

Base in the skunk with the No. 4 and Paynes Gray + Burnt Umber for the darks and Ultra White + Cobalt Blue for the white area. Again use the flat edge of the brush to flip the paint into the background to give the look of fur. Flip the white over the black part. **DO NOT DO THE TAIL YET.**

LOG

Add some highlights on the log with Burnt Umber + Unbleached Titanium and add some darks with Burnt Umber + Paynes Gray. Add some touches of Misty Gray on the log behind the tail.

SKUNK

Use the No. 4 chisel edge and Paynes Gray + Burnt Umber. Paint in the end of the tail, being sure to keep the end hair loose. Add some Misty Gray and paint in the middle section of the tail still using the chisel edge of the brush. Next add the dark area at the base of the tail. Use the liner brush and Misty Gray + Cobalt Blue and add some fine hair on the tip of the tail. Add some Ultra White hairs. Add some Ivory Black at the base of the tail. Contour the body with Ivory Black and add highlight with Misty Gray + Cobalt Blue. Add some hair strokes in the white areas and use the liner to paint in some fine white hair over the black hair. Outline the eye with Ivory Black and add the eyelid with Misty Gray + Burnt Umber. Add the highlight on the nose with this color also. Add a touch of Brilliant Yellow Light to highlight the eye and nose.

FINISHING

When the Painting is dry it may be sprayed with Jenkins Sta-Brite Varnish.

"FLOWER"

"SKIPPY THE GRAY SQUIRREL"

"Skippy the Gray Squirrel"

CANVAS: 8 x 10 Glenice Canvas or Portrait Quality Canvas

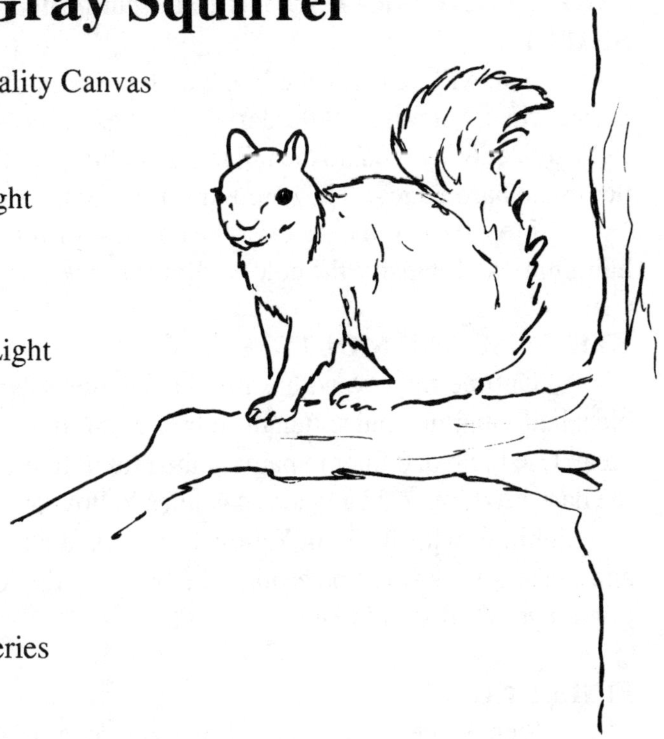

PALETTE

Ultra White
Unbleached Titanium
Burnt Sienna
Paynes Gray
Yellow Citron
Deep Orange
Cobalt Blue
Brilliant Yellow Light
Raw Sienna
Burnt Umber
Naples Yellow
Cadmium Yellow Light
Sap Green

BRUSHES

No. 24 Royal Superb Blend
Nos. 2, 4, and 6 Loew Cornell 797-F Series
No. 0 Loew Cornell Mixtique Liner 8050 Series
1 Inch and 1/2 Inch Langnickle Skywash 1357 Series
Binney-Smith 55-11 Palette Knife

MEDIUM

Zec Gel - used to texture the tree trunk. It is not necessary for you to use this product if you choose not to. The tree may be painted in using the colors that are listed in the lesson plan . Just omit the Zec Gel.

Odorless Turpentine - You will need one container to clean your brushes in and a small container to keep by your palette to be used to thin your paint.

DIRECTIONS

1. Read the sections "General Painting Tips" and "How To Start Your Painting".
2. Read the instructions all of the way through before you transfer the pattern on to the canvas.

BACKGROUND

Use the No. 24 Royal and a mixture of Ultra White + Cobalt Blue to paint in the sky. Paint around the leaf shapes. Use very little paint. Base in the leaf shapes with Sap Green + Yellow Citron + Unbleached Titanium and Cadmium Yellow Light + Deep Orange and Deep Orange + Burnt Sienna and Burnt Sienna + Burnt Umber. Use the No. 2 chisel edge and all of the colors that you used to base in the leaf shapes to highlight. Work in lighter and darker values on each leaf and use Paynes Gray for the very dark areas. Use the Skywash to soften.

TREE

Mix Burnt Umber + Paynes Gray together and use the palette knife to chop in the Zec. Do not mash the Zec into the paint. Make a bead of paint along the edge of the knife and lay in the bark of the tree. Add some Ultra White to the mixture and lay in the branches behind the squirrel. Pull the knife around the branch. Smooth the paint out as it nears where the squirrels tail will go. Mix some Raw Sienna + Naples Yellow and apply the highlights on the bark. This step should be done after the dark layer has dried. You may want to add some color to the bark with some transparent washes.

"SKIPPY THE GRAY SQUIRREL" continued

SKIPPY

You will be using the No. 2 and 4 to paint in the squirrel. Start with a wash of Burnt Umber + Unbleached Titanium. Add darks with base mix + Paynes Gray. Use Unbleached Titanium for the light areas. When you do the tail use a dry brush to flip the tail hair into the background. Remember do not make hard edges. They are almost impossible to cover later. This is Step One.

Step Two: Go back over the entire squirrel with the chisel edge of the No. 2 brush and paint in hair clumps. Intensify the colors. Refer to the reference picture.

EYE, NOSE AND MOUTH

Outline the eye with a mixture of Burnt Umber + Paynes Gray. Add the outer layer of Unbleached Titanium and soften the edge. Paint in the Unbleached Titanium on the cheeks and the mouth area. Use the No. 0 liner to paint in the mouth line with the dark mix and soften. Paint in the nose with the dark mixture. Add a touch of Naples Yellow on the tip of the nose. Fill in the eye with the dark mix and highlight with Brilliant Yellow Light. Add a tiny touch of Ultra White to the tip of the liner brush and make a very fine line around the bottom edge of the eye (on the dark paint). This will make the lower eyelid. It should be rather faint.

FINISHING

Step Three: Use the #0 Liner and paint in some fine hair. Be careful not to overdo this step. Add some Deep Orange in the highlight areas on the body. Highlight these with Naples Yellow and then with Brilliant Yellow Light. Add some Brilliant Yellow Light to highlight the light area on the hind leg. Add some light and dark hairs in the tail. The rear paw is Unbleached Titanium + Burnt Umber. Separate the toes with a darker value. The front paw is Unbleached Titanium + Paynes Gray. Separate the toes with Burnt Umber.

When the painting is dry to the touch it may be sprayed with a protective coating of Jenkins Sta-Brite Varnish.

Susan Scheewe Publications, Inc.

ACRYLIC BOOKS

	Vol.	Title	No.	Price
	Vol. 19	"Gift of Painting" by Susan Scheewe	230	$9.50
	Vol. 1	"Painting It's Our Bag" by Bev Hink/Susan Scheewe	193	$9.50
	Vol. 4	"Keepsake Sampler" by Susan & Camille Scheewe	200	$9.50
	Vol. 1	"Loving You" by Susan & Camille Scheewe	244	$9.50
	Vol. 1	"Keepsakes For The Holidays" by Charleen Stempel & Susan Scheewe	286	$9.50
	Vol. 1	"Mrs. MacGregor's Garden" by Charleen Stempel & Susan Scheewe	316	$9.50
	Vol. 1	"Kids And Water" by Joyce Benner	234	$9.50
	Vol. 2	"The Flower Market" by Joyce Benner	319	$9.50
	Vol. 1	"Natures Palette" by Carol Binford	248	$9.50
	Vol. 1	"Country Fixin's" by Rhonda Caldwell	307	$9.50
	Vol. 2	"Country Fixin's - Sunflower Friends" by Rhonda Caldwell	321	$9.50
*NEW	Vol. 3	"Country Fixin's - For All Seasons" by Rhonda Caldwell	332	$9.50
	Vol. 1	"Santas and Sams" by Bobi Dolara	258	$9.50
	Vol. 2	"Vintage Peace" by Bobi Dolara	270	$9.50
	Vol. 1	"Floral Designs" by Carol Empet	312	$9.50
*NEW	Vol. 2	"Floral Designs 2" by Carol Empet	338	$9.50
	Vol. 1	"Romantically Tole Bauernmalerei" by Sherry Gall	311	$9.50
	Vol. 1	"Holiday Gathering" by Angie Hupp	267	$9.50
	Vol. 3	"Heavenly Gathering" by Angie Hupp	320	$9.50
	Vol. 1	"Happy Heart, Happy Home" by Cathy Jones	241	$9.50
	Vol. 1	"Pickets & Pastimes" by Marie & Jim King	329	$9.50
*NEW	Vol. 2	"Pickets & Pastimes 2, Heart of The Seasons" by Marie & Jim King	348	$9.50
	Vol. 1	"Huckleberry Horse" by Hanna Long	269	$9.50
	Vol. 1	"Love Lives Here" by Mary Lynn Lewis	170	$6.50
	Vol. 2	"Love Lives Here" by Mary Lynn Lewis	185	$6.50
	Vol. 3	"Love Lives Here" by Mary Lynn Lewis	195	$6.50
	Vol. 1	"Special Welcomes" by Corinne Miller	287	$9.50
	Vol. 2	"Special Welcomes" by Corinne Miller	298	$9.50
	Vol. 3	"Special Welcomes #3, Crazy About Crafting" by Corinne Miller	309	$9.50
	Vol. 4	"Special Welcomes #4 Farm-N-Friends" by Corinne Miller	324	$9.50
*NEW	Vol. 5	"Special Welcomes #5 All Wrapped Up" by Corinne Miller	333	$9.50
*NEW	Vol. 6	"Special Welcomes #6 Crop Keepers" by Corinne Miller	347	$9.50
	Vol. 1	"Change With The Seasons, Wire Loops" by Joanna Miller	331	$9.50
	Vol. 1	"Fruit & Flower Fantasies" by Joyce Morrison	277	$9.50
	Vol. 1	"Wildflower Sampler" by Bev Norman	191	$9.50
	Vol. 1	"Whimsical Critters" by Lori Ohlson	228	$7.50
	Vol. 2	"Sunflower Farm" by Lori Ohlson	326	$9.50
	Vol. 1	"Holiday Medley" by Nina Owens	265	$9.50
	Vol. 2	"Another Holiday Medley" by Nina Owens	296	$9.50
	Vol. 1	"Oh Those Little Rascals" by Diane Permenter	247	$9.50
	Vol. 6	"Acrylic Charms" by Sharon Rachal	305	$9.50
	Vol. 1	"Forever In My Heart" by Diane Richards.....AC/Fabric	188	$6.50
	Vol. 2	"Memories In My Heart" by Diane Richards.....AC/Fabric	189	$6.50
	Vol. 3	"Forever In My Heart II" by Diane Richards.....AC/Fabric	205	$9.50
	Vol. 6	"Angels In My Stocking" by Diane Richards	254	$9.50
	Vol. 7	"Nostalgic Dreams" by Diane Richards	273	$9.50
*NEW	Vol. 8	"Angel Kisses" by Diane Richards	346	$9.50
	Vol. 1	"Holiday Hangarounds" by Marsha Sellers	327	$9.50
	Vol. 1	"Creations In Canvas...and More" by Carol Spooner	256	$9.50
	Vol. 1	"Gran's Garden" by Ros Stallcup	295	$9.50
	Vol. 2	"Another Gran's Garden" by Ros Stallcup	315	$9.50
*NEW	Vol. 3	"Gran's Garden & House" by Ros Stallcup	334	$9.50
*NEW	Vol. 4	"Gran's Garden Party" by Ros Stallcup	345	$9.50
*NEW	Vol. 1	"Christmas Greetings from the Cottage" by Chris Stokes	336	$9.50
	Vol. 2	"Christmas Presence" by Max Terry	285	$9.50
	Vol. 3	"Painting Clay Pot-pourri" by Max Terry	310	$9.50
	Vol. 1	"Country Primitives" by Maxine Thomas	274	$9.50
	Vol. 2	"Country Primitives 2" by Maxine Thomas	300	$9.50
	Vol. 3	"Country Primitives 3" by Maxine Thomas	322	$9.50
	Vol. 1	"Rise & Shine" by Jolene Thompson	214	$6.50
	Vol. 2	"Garden Gate" by Jolene Thompson	250	$9.50
	Vol. 3	"Count Your Blessings" by Chris Thornton	196	$6.50
	Vol. 5	"Count Your Blessings" by Chris Thornton	213	$0.50
	Vol. 6	"Share Your Blessings" by Chris Thornton	226	$0.50
	Vol. 7	"Blessings" by Chris Thornton	255	$9.50
	Vol. 8	"Christmas Blessings" by Chris Thornton	266	$9.50
	Vol. 9	"Blessings For The Home" by Chris Thornton	275	$9.50
	Vol. 10	"Bazaar Blessings" by Chris Thornton	299	$9.50
	Vol. 11	"Painted Blessings" by Chris Thornton	323	$9.50
*NEW	Vol. 1	"Watermelon Wedges and Rustic Edges" by Lorinne Thurlow	342	$9.50
	Vol. 1	"Barnyard Friends" by Lou Ann Trice	306	$9.50
	Vol. 5	"Daydreams & Sweet Shirts II" by Don & Lynn Weed	208	$9.50
*NEW	Vol. 1	"Connie's Favorite Old-Time Labels" by Connie Williams	335	$9.50
	Vol. 1	"Floral Fabrics and Watercolor" by Sally Williams	262	$9.50
	Vol. 1	"A Time For Giving" by Evelyn Wright	308	$9.50

****

SHIPPING & HANDLING CHARGES

Add $2.50 for the First Book for shipping and handling.

Add $1.50 per each additional book.

Please Add $3.00 for handling & postage. PER TAPES. Sorry we must have a "NO REFUND - NO RETURN" policy.

U.S CURRENCY

PRICES SUBJECT TO CHANGE WITHOUT NOTICE

FOR MORE INFORMATION ON BOOKS OR SUPPLIES CALL OR WRITE US

WE ARE ALWAYS GLAD TO HEAR FROM YOU!

3-1-96

13435 N.E. Whitaker Way Portland, Or. 97230 PH(503)254-9100 FAX(503)252-9508

WATERCOLOR BOOKS

	Vol.	Title	No.	Price	Qty
	Vol. 20	"Simply Country Watercolors" by Susan Scheewe Brown	257	$9.50	___
	Vol. 21	"Simply Watercolor" by Susan Scheewe Brown.....T.V. Book	260	$11.95	___
	Vol. 22	"Watercolor For Everyone" by Susan Scheewe Brown.....T.V. Book	276	$11.95	___
	Vol. 23	"Watercolor Step by Step" by Susan Scheewe Brown.....T.V. Book	294	$11.95	___
	Vol. 24	"Introduction to Watercolor" by Susan Scheewe Brown.....T.V. Book	314	$11.95	___
	Vol. 25	"Watercolors Anyone Can Paint" by Susan Scheewe Brown...T.V. Book	325	$11.95	___
*NEW	Vol. 26	"Watercolor - The Garden Scene" by Susan Scheewe Brown... T.V. Book	341	$11.95	___
	Vol. 4	"Enjoy Watercolor" by Ellie Cook	210	$7.50	___
	Vol. 6	"Watercolor Memories" by Ellie Cook	246	$9.50	___
	Vol. 7	"My Favorite Things In Watercolor" by Ellie Cook	293	$9.50	___
	Vol. 3	"Watercolor Made Easy 3" by Kathy George	301	$9.50	___
	Vol. 1	"The Way I Started" by Gary Hawk	120	$6.00	___
	Vol. 2	"Anyone Can Watercolor" by Ken Johnson	118	$6.50	___
	Vol. 1	"Watercolor Fun & Easy" by Beverly Kaiser	243	$7.50	___
	Vol. 1	"Flowers, Ribbon and Lace in Watercolor" by Linda McCulloch	280	$9.50	___

PEN & INK BOOKS / COLORED PENCIL BOOKS

Vol.	Title	No.	Price	Qty
Vol. 6	"Journey of Memories" by Claudia Nice	166	$6.50	___
Vol. 7	"Scenes from Seasons Past" by Claudia Nice	183	$9.50	___
Vol. 8	"Taste of Summer" by Claudia Nice	223	$9.50	___
Vol. 9	"Familiar Faces" by Claudia Nice	284	$9.50	___
Vol. 2	"Colored Pencil Made Easy" by Jane Wunder	242	$7.50	___
Vol. 3	"The Beauty of Colored Pencil and Ink Drawing" by Jane Wunder	259	$7.50	___

VIDEOS BY SUSAN SCHEEWE BROWN

Title	Price	Qty
"The Gift Of Painting Simply Watercolor" 60 Minutes	$24.95	___
"The Gift Of Painting" 90 Minutes	$24.95	___
"Paintings For The Holidays" 60 Minutes	$24.95	___
"Watercolor & Oil Do Mix" 60 Minutes	$24.95	___
"Watercolor Special Effects" 60 Minutes	$24.95	___

- NAME ______________
- ______________
- ADDRESS ______________
- ______________
- CITY/STATE/ZIP ______________
- ______________
- PH( ) ______________
- VISA ______________
- M/C ______________
- EXP. DATE ______________
- SHIPPING $ ______________
- SHIP TO ______________
- ______________
- ______________

OILS BOOKS

Vol.	Title	No.	Price	Qty
Vol. 1	"His and Hers" by Susan Scheewe	101	$6.50	___
Vol. 6	"Brushed With Elegance" by Susan Scheewe	106	$9.50	___
Vol. 7	"Paint 'n Patch" by Susan Scheewe	107	$5.50	___
Vol. 11	"I Love To Paint" by Susan Scheewe	111	$9.50	___
Vol. 14	"Enjoy Painting Animals" by Susan Scheewe	114	$9.50	___
Vol. 17	"Countryside Reflections" by Susan Scheewe	161	$6.50	___
Vol. 19	"Gift Of Painting" by Susan Scheewe O/AC/WC	230	$9.50	___
Vol. 1	"Western Images" by Becky Anthony	186	$6.50	___
Vol. 3	"Fantasy Flowers II" by Georgia Bartlett	129	$6.50	___
Vol. 5	"Soft Petals" by Georgia Bartlett	171	$6.50	___
Vol. 6	"Painting Fantasy Flowers" by Georgia Bartlett	215	$7.50	___
Vol. 7	"Flowers" by Georgia Bartlett	290	$9.50	___
Vol. 8	"Petals" by Georgia Bartlett	317	$9.50	___
Vol. 9	"Floral Medley" by Georgia Bartlett ....*NEW..	344	$9.50	___
Vol. 3	"Barnscapes & More" by Donna Bell	218	$9.50	___
Vol. 4	"Countryscapes" by Donna Bell	249	$9.50	___
Vol. 5	"Painter to Painter" by Donna Bell	263	$9.50	___
Vol. 6	"Landscapes With Acrylics & Oil" by Donna Bell	282	$9.50	___
Vol. 1	"Natures Palette" by Carol Binford.....O/AC	248	$9.50	___
Vol. 1	"Oil Painting The Easy Way" by Bill Blackman	219	$9.50	___
Vol. 2	"Oil Painting The Easy Way" by Bill Blackman .....*NEW.	337	$9.50	___
Vol. 1	"Mini Mini More" by Terri and Nancy Brown	150	$9.50	___
Vol. 2	"Mini Mini More" by Terri and Nancy Brown	151	$9.50	___
Vol. 4	"Heritage Trails" by Terri and Nancy Brown	169	$6.50	___
Vol. 6	"Garden Trails" by Terri and Nancy Brown	283	$9.50	___
Vol. 2	"Windows of My World" by Jackie Claflin	181	$9.50	___
Vol. 3	"Windows of My World 3" by Jackie Claflin	303	$9.50	___
Vol. 4	"Expressions In Oil" by Delores Egger	239	$7.50	___
Vol. 1	"Victorian Days" by Gloria Gaffney	240	$9.50	___
Vol. 2	"Days of Heaven" by Gloria Gaffney	252	$9.50	___
Vol. 3	"Winter Song" by Gloria Gaffney	271	$9.50	_
Vol. 1	"Roses Are For Everyone" by Bill Huffaker	145	$9.50	_
Vol. 3	"Nature's Beauty" by Bill Huffaker	177	$6.50	_
Vol. 1	"Copper, Silver, Brass & Glass" by Susan Jenkins	211	$6.50	_
Vol. 1	"In Full Bloom" by Susan Jenkins	313	$9.50	_
Vol. 1	"Backroads of My Memory" by Geri Kisner	225	$9.50	_
Vol. 2	"Backroads of My Memory" by Geri Kisner	245	$9.50	_
Vol. 1	"Ducks and Geese" by Jean Lyles	172	$6.50	_
Vol. 1	"Raining Cats & Dogs" by Todd Mallett	304	$9.50	_
Vol. 1	"Pathway To Painting" by Lee McGowan	281	$9.50	_
Vol. 2	"Another Path To Follow" by Lee McGowen	328	$9.50	_
Vol. 1	"Bitterroot Backroads" by Glenice Moore	330	$9.50	_
Vol. 2	"Bitteroot Backroads 2" by Glenice Moore.........*NEW.	340	$9.50	_
Vol. 1	"Stepping Stones" by Judy Nutter	121	$6.50	_
Vol. 1	"Painting with Paulson" by Buck Paulson..........*NEW.	343	$11.95	_
Vol. 1	"Rustic Charms" by Sharon Rachal	175	$6.50	_
Vol. 2	"Rustic Charms II" by Sharon Rachal	199	$9.50	_
Vol. 3	"Rustic Charms III" by Sharon Rachal	217	$6.50	_
Vol. 4	"Rustic Charms IV" by Sharon Rachal	238	$7.50	_
Vol. 5	"Rustic Charms V, Florals" by Sharon Rachal	261	$9.50	_
Vol. 1	"Painting Flowers With Augie" by Augie Reis	152	$6.50	_
Vol. 2	"Painting Realism" by Judy Sleight	272	$9.50	_
Vol. 3	"Realistic Technique" by Judy Sleight..............*NEW...	341	$9.50	_
Vol. 1	"Soft & Misty Paintings" by Kathy Snider	204	$9.50	_
Vol. 2	"Soft & Misty Paintings"by Kathy Snider	229	$9.50	_
Vol. 4	"Friends We've Known" by Gene Waggoner	187	$7.50	_
Vol. 5	"Friends Are Forever" by Gene Waggoner	231	$7.50	_
Vol. 1	"Fantasy Folk" by Don Weed	123	$6.50	_
Vol. 2	"Painting The Clowns" by Don Weed	124	$6.50	_
Vol. 1	"Something Special For Everyone" by Mildred Yeiser	158	$6.50	_
Vol. 2	"Something Special For Everyone" by Mildred Yeiser	178	$6.50	_
Vol. 5	"Soft & Gentle Paintings" by Mildred Yeiser	268	$9.50	_

Susan Scheewe Publications Inc.

13435 N.E. Whitaker Way Portland, Or. 97230 PH (503) 254-9100 FAX (503) 252-9508